New Talmudic Readings

New TALMUDIC READINGS

EMMANUEL LEVINAS

TRANSLATED BY
RICHARD A. COHEN

DUQUESNE UNIVERSITY PRESS
PITTSBURGH, PA 15282

First published in French in 1996 under the title
Nouvelles Lectures Talmudiques
Copyright © by Les Editions de Minuit

English Translation Copyright © 1999 by Duquesne University Press
Introduction Copyright © 1999 by Richard A. Cohen
All rights reserved.

Published in the United States of America
by Duquesne University Press
600 Forbes Avenue
Pittsburgh, PA 15282

Library of Congress Cataloging in Publication Data

Levinas, Emmanuel.
     [Nouvelles lectures talmudiques. English]
     New Talmudic readings / by Emmanuel Levinas; translated by
Richard A. Cohen.
        p.   cm.
     Includes bibliographical references and index.
     ISBN 0–8207–0297–8 (cloth: alk. paper)
     1. Talmud—Theology.   2. Talmud—Criticism, interpretation, etc.
3. Bible. O.T.—Criticism, interpretation, etc., Jewish.   I. Cohen,
Richard A., 1950–   II. Title.
     BM504.3 .L486   1999
     296.1'2506—dc21
                                                            99–6128
                                                            CIP

Printed on acid-free paper.

Contents

Translator's Notes

Quotations from the Bible remain faithful primarily to Levinas's French translations, but standard English translations have also been consulted and have to some extent been integrated into the English translation. Specific references to Talmud and to Bible verses and lines in the English translation occasionally reflect corrections of erroneous references given in the French text. Talmud translations remain faithful primarily to Levinas's French translations, but two English Talmud translations (Soncino and Brown Judaic Studies) have also been consulted and have to some extent been integrated into the English translation. Regarding various names of God: *"Dieu"* is translated as "God," *"Eternal"* and *"Seigneur"* are both translated as "Lord." In addition, I have retained the gender-specific language used in Levinas's original French texts.

SOME NOTES ON THE TEXTS

These three Talmudic readings were first delivered as keynote addresses at the annual Colloquium of French-Speaking Jewish Intellectuals. "The Will of God and the Power of Humanity" was delivered in November 1974, at the Colloquium whose general topic was "Solitude in Israel." Like Levinas's previous addresses, and all but two of his subsequent addresses, it was published afterwards, appearing in this case in *L'Herne: Emmanuel Levinas*, edited by Catherine Chalier and Migeul Abensour (Paris: Editions de L'Herne, 1991), pp. 120–33. A note under the title in the present volume indicates that this address was also delivered to the central Consistory, the official government-supported Jewish administrative body of the Jewish community of France.

"Beyond the State in the State" was delivered in December 1988, at the annual Colloquium whose general topic was "Question of the State." "Who is One-Self?" was delivered in December 1989, at the annual Colloquium whose general topic was "As-for-Oneself." Levinas gave keynote addresses at no less than 25 of the colloquia of French-speaking Jewish intellectuals, from 1959 to 1989. (For a complete list of Levinas's presentations, see Robert Gibbs, *Correlations in Rosenzweig and Levinas* [Princeton: Princeton University Press, 1992], 175). "Beyond the State in the State" (1988) and "Who is One-Self?" (1989) were published posthumously in the French volume—entitled *Nouvelles Lectures Talmudiques* (Paris: Editions de Minuit, 1996)—of which the present volume is the English translation.

Levinas passed away in Paris at the age of 88 on December 25, 1994. Hence these latter two texts represent Levinas's last two Talmudic readings. A caution: not only their late date, their posthumous publication, and their relative brevity, but also certain textual ambiguities, certain grammatical and semantic irregularities and abbreviations, including missing verbs and articles, all lead me to believe that both texts, and especially the last, are to some extent unedited or underedited manuscripts—that is to say, working notes or lecture notes, rather than the precise and polished works which are the hallmark of Levinas's own published writings, including the 1974 reading contained herein. Regretable and inconvenient as the lacunae contained in them may prove, however, the originality and perspicacity of Levinas's thought nonetheless clearly shines through, or so it seems to me.

Humanism, Religion, Myth, Criticism, Exegesis

This introductory essay is guided by two related aims. At its core it aims to explicate the nature and value of the ethico-exegetical approach at work in Emmanuel Levinas's three Talmudic readings, as elsewhere in his writings. Exegesis, in Levinas's hands, signifies far more than what one might ordinarily expect from a method or technique of textual analysis. The second aim of this introduction, then, is to elucidate the larger issues at stake by locating Levinas's exegetical approach, both critically and positively, within the broader ethical-metaphysical project of biblical humanism that drives Levinas's thought as a whole, and represents his proper contribution to contemporary thought. Though Levinas is certainly mindful that the texts he is commenting upon are chosen from the heart and soul of Jewish tradition, from the Talmud and (through the Talmud) the Bible, his readings are an affair neither for Jews or Judaism alone, nor for spiritually inclined individuals and religious communities alone—large and important as these intended audiences are. The significance of Levinas's readings is universal, for all the world.

BIBLICAL HUMANISM

Levinas—and not only Levinas—has been accused of humanism. As if this were an accusation! Who are the accusers? What is the fault? Martin Heidegger, fresh from the horrors of the Nazi experience, fresh from *his own* 12-year Nazi Party membership, unapologetic, chose to denounce humanism two years after war's end in his famous 1947 "Letter on Humanism." Not in the excesses of fascism, or mechanized impersonal war, or mass death, or the leveling of Rotterdam, Dresden, Hiroshima, or the Rape of Nanjing, or slave labor camps, or the crematoria at Auschwicz, but in humanism, of all things, would Heidegger discover the scourge of human willfulness, self-assertion, loss of being. Humanism would be held accountable not for an appreciation, however poorly actualized, of the humanity of the human,—the "universal rights of man," as it promised—but rather for the terminal closure of ontological horizons brought about by a technological worldview triumphant beyond anyone's dreams, the nightmare. So much for the celebrated subtleties of *Denken*. In America, concerned with an altogether different transcendence, religious fundamentalists would rant against the evils of "secular humanism," condemned as prideful and godless, adulating the human while heedless of the divine. Scientific discoveries, biblical criticism, religious ecumenism and social idealism would all be lumped together and scorned as Satanic. One reels from these peculiar accusations, from their perversity. What strange bedfellows antihumanism makes: the German philosopher Heidegger (and his disciples) and American religious fundamentalists.

In the face of a global, perennial, and well-documented history of inhumanities—slavery, serfdom, economic and political disenfranchisement, repression, war, suppression of women and minorities, colonialism, mass starvation, torture, imperialism, genocide, tyranny, etc.—Can it really be humanism that is at fault? Can any stretch of reasoning or imagination, however adroit, convince us that humanism is to be lamented and denounced for being the root cause and culmination of barbarism, rather than its enemy? This seems far too clever, another case of the intellect's penchant for novel and simple explanations, for an oblivious but superior self-absorption, for arcane conspiracy theories—in a word, for losing perspective. Is it not possible, even likely, actually the very case, that precisely the reverse is true? Humanism—by which I mean, at the very least, a pragmatic and fundamental respect for the irreducible dignity and worth of each and every human being *qua* human being—is it not rather a great human good, and hence indirectly also a great *religious* good? Even more, is not humanism directly a religious good, perhaps even the highest, the greatest of religious goods, the very vocation of the individual as *homo re-ligiosus*, of humanity consecrated to the task of returning to God? Such is the case Levinas will make in these three Talmudic readings, and elsewhere in his other Talmudic readings, as well as in his philosophy as a whole. Humanity is not duped, but elevated, by morality.

For Levinas, humanism, respect for the human *qua* human, does not derive from or remain limited to some Greek or Renaissance or Enlightenment "definition" of the human being: "rational animal," "worker," "artist," "homo sapien," "homo politicus," "language user." Rather, more deeply, it recalls and animates a central biblical teaching: the idea— and not *merely* an idea—that each and every human being, regardless of differences in wealth, power, talent, position or status, is "created" in "the image and likeness of God." Though it may be incomprehensible, the trace of transcendence finds its way into the hearts of all humanity. All humans and a humanity so dedicated, across the diversity of individuals, families and nations—despite but not wholly indifferent to these distinctions as well as to historical differences in military, political, economic and cultural achievements—is, in a profoundly meaningful sense, one humanity. This one global human community stretches beyond families, friends, neighbors and fellow citizens, welcoming complete strangers, even enemies, binding together near and far, rich and poor, strong and weak, healthy and sick, ally and enemy, fortunate and wretched, good and evil. Here lie thick and complex concatenations of meanings and imperatives—significance and not merely signification—worthy not only of thought but of life. The Bible expresses this unity—universal fellowship, universal humanity, the humanity of the human, fraternity—not in the rational and exclusionary discursiveness of philosophical exposition, nor merely in the quasi-scientific terms of the biological and hence racist parentage of an Adam and Eve, or Noah and Naama, or finally of Abraham and Sarah. Rather, the Bible describes the outstanding ethico-spiritual attributes of truth, righteousness, hospitality and compassion that these biblical figures do not merely represent or understand or declaim, but which they live and breathe and walk in the concrete and inspirational narratives of the Bible. Paradigmatic narratives. Here one finds loftiness with its feet on the ground, a human sensitivity attentive at once to heights and failings, to failings measured by heights. Is not the Bible as much a record of human failings as of human achievements, and as such a unique document in the spiritual order of the world? Neither a human comedy nor a human tragedy—for who stands outside looking in?—but a human community, united under the just and merciful "eyes" of an invisible but inescapable God.

Just as Heidegger's penetrating critique of "onto-theology" unmasks the forced and illusory *mythologizing* inherent in religious primitivism (including its secular forms), such as is all too often found in American fundamentalism with its dogmatic spiritual diremptions and its contagious veneration of a being within being as the Supreme Being, so too Hans Jonas has with no less penetration shown the latent *paganism* of Heidegger's suggested alternative, his "turn" (*Kehre*), his entranced and entrancing pontifications calling for a heightened attunement to the no less exclusionary oracular (verbal) be-ing of beings. Paganism, Jonas warns, lies not merely in some dark and distant origin, overcome once and for all, but rather in the winking complacency of a being all too certain of its own being-in-and-of-the-world.[1] That this seductive appeal of the earth, as it were, continues to haunt and challenge civilization had already been shown by Franz Rosenzweig in his great religious work *The Star of Redemption* (1921). Levinas first warned of it in 1934 in a short article modestly entitled "Some Reflections on the Philosophy of Hitlerism,"[2] But the critique of the immanentist and totalizing mythologies of both "onto-theology," the divinization of a being, and the divinization of *be-ing* itself, began neither with Heidegger nor with Jonas, nor with Bultmann, Buber, Rosenzweig or Nietzsche, nor with the rationally definitive and devastating aporia articulated in the Dialectic of Kant's

---

[1] For references to Hans Jonas's writings and further discussion of the question of paganism in Heidegger, see my *Elevations: The Height of the Good in Rosenzweig and Levinas* (Chicago: University of Chicago Press, 1994), 300–04.

[2] Emmanuel Levinas, "Quelques reflexions sur la philosophie de l'hitlerism," *Esprit*, 2, No. 26 (November 1934): 199–208.

Critique of Pure Reason, nor with Hume's urbane but hyperbolic skepticism, nor even with the "negative theology," the "God without being," of a Thomas Aquinas, as read, say, by Jean-Luc Marion. Nor did a genuine humanism have to wait centuries for Paul's declaration that in Christ "there is neither Jew nor Greek, there is neither slave nor free, there is neither male nor female," in Colossians 3.19. Rather, far earlier, out of an "immemorial past" at the very dawn of history—and always, at every moment, here, now, "in the beginning" of a continual dawning of history, out of an immemorial past whose immemoriality traces an insecurity in the heart of being upon which history dawns—humanism begins with traditions as ancient, in the West, as the Hebraic. This tradition reveals a God who is both uniquely one, at once immanent and transcendent, and for the same reason uniquely invisible, beyond being and essence, and more present than the presence of the present. The idea of such a beginning, ancient yet contemporary, a more in a less, whose peculiar time structure Levinas will call "diachrony," is immediately disturbing, excessive, provocative, unsettling—to all the powers that be.

The imperialism of ancient Rome—and all that is still represented by such a "Rome," that is to say, by imperialism, by statism, by the overt and subtle powers of the powers that be—was outraged to find that within the innermost precinct of the great Jewish Temple in Jerusalem—a Temple at once spiritual and material; an ancient architectural "wonder of the world" and a spiritual wonder of all worlds; a building, with many courtyards and sanctuaries, with many elevations, surrounded and supported by the massive stone bulwarks which stand to this day—in its very heart and soul, in a chamber known as the "Holy of Holies," a *place* (Hebrew: *makom*, a term which is one of God's "names"!), there stood no icon, no statue, no oracle, no god, no image, nothing. There was only a box containing the hewn tablets of the Ten Commandments given to Moses, to the Jewish people, and to all the nations of the world, at Mount Sinai.

A temple without an idol—an outrage to pagan sensibilities. Furthermore, the tablets in the Holy of Holies were *not* the tablets of the Ten Commandments given by God to Moses on Mount Sinai. The Bible, in its near obsessive honesty, does not flinch from informing its readers of the first tablets that they were destroyed by Moses at the foot of Mount Sinai in response to the idol worship of God's own people (and here Israel is certainly a paradigm for all humanity). Many paintings attempt to depict this striking and awesome moment, the breaking of the first tablets. Carved and given by God, inscribed by God the first tablets were smashed. Thus when God's commandments were presented to Israel they were "preoriginal" from the start. Just as the Bible begins with the second letter of the aleph-bet, and the Talmud has no first page, the tablets sheltered in the Temple were, from the very first, second.

The shattered first tablets were *too first*, as it were, too exalted, cut too far above the measure of humanity. The Midrash tells that their letters returned to heaven, leaving behind tablets too heavy for Moses to bear. In the short time of the first tablets, given on high on the shrouded mountaintop above, in the plains far below the Jews persuaded themselves to imitate the idol worship of pagans, forming and worshipping a "golden calf." Too pure a divinity yields only a debased humanity. The high and the low would have to be brought into conjunction, into unequal reciprocity; *religion (re-ligio)* would henceforth be necessary for the very humanity of the human and the divinity of the divine. Distances—one of the topics Levinas discusses apropos a conversation between

Alexander the Great and the Rabbis of the Negev, in the second Talmudic reading herein—must be bridged. Paradoxically, the transcendent God must transcend God's own transcendence. Religion and humanism, then, would arise together in the warmth of *rachmanes*, a Hebrew term which means "compassion," "mercy," and whose root forms the letters of the word for "womb," and is also yet another of God's names. Isaiah 57.15: "I abide in exaltedness and holiness—but am with the contrite and lowly of spirit, to revive the spirit of the lowly and to revive the heart of the contrite."[3] Religion would require of humans neither a blind obedience nor an alienated freedom, but rather the "difficult freedom" of biblical humanism, neither too high nor too low, neither ashes nor ice.

In the Temple's Holy of Holies, in the Ark of the Covenant, were kept the second tablets of the Ten Commandments, commandments in which one could rejoice, commandments one could both "remember" and "keep," both "follow" and "obey," despite failures, lapses, backsliding, "bad conscience," and the concomitant constant need for repentance. Humans—neither devils nor angels, hence capable of both good and evil—would be "given" a Torah, would enter into relationship with a forgiving and just God. In the first Talmudic reading of this volume, entitled "The Will of God and the Power of Humanity," Levinas will try to understand and to show how divine commandments, executed through carefully regulated

---

[3] For an interpretation of Isaiah and other Hebrew prophets, one cannot recommend too highly Abraham Joshua Heschel, *The Prophets*, vols. 1 & 2 (New York: Harper & Row, 1962). On pages 95 of vol. 2, just to make one brief citation, Heschel writes: "Compassion is the root of God's relationship to man." *God's* relationship to man!

and humane judicial proceedings, are no less than divine *rewards* and not simply divine retribution. The commandments of the second tablets were the same commandments as the first, to be sure, but the stones of the second were carved and contributed by Moses, not by God (though still according to God's command). The significance of this difference has too often been overlooked. Coming second, taking second place, the other-before-the-self, the other-put-into-the-same, converts firstness—the for-oneself, *of both God and humanity*—into an actual *relationship*, the most concrete and pressing of relationships, the exigencies of morality and justice, breaking the bounds of both terms. Abraham—first of the Jews, by God's command—is he who challenges even God according to God's own justice. Not abjection but election.

Relationship with God—covenant—henceforth would involve two heterogeneous times: preoriginal or "immemorial" time, and a disrupted present, troubled, put upon, overburdened, obligated. This is the time of "diachrony," link and rupture at once, the temporality of a "present" always already too late even "in the beginning," burst by a past too past, and, demanded by that very immemorial past, a future too future, what Levinas at the end of *Totality and Infinity* calls "messianic time, where the perpetual is converted into the eternal."[4] Diachrony is no less the conjunction of two heterogeneous parties or partners: God and humankind. God is brought down to the earth upon which humans live and breath and walk, and humans are raised to their proper stature, raised to heavenly heights serving God through His commands. Just as the divine disappears in human arrogance

---

4 Emmanuel Levinas, *Totality and Infinity*, trans. Alphonso Lingis (Pittsburgh: Duquesne University Press, 1969), 285.

(the warranted complaint of fundamentalists, Heidegger, and all the religious traditions), so too humanity—the humanity and dignity of the human—disappears in an excessive absoluteness attributed to the mastery of God. Already this complex dialectic—two times, two partners, and two registers of significance, the intertwining of being and morality, heterogeneous yet making contact—is contained, for exegesis, in the allegedly simple "Bible story" of the two sets of tablets of the Ten Commandments.

A modern reader of the Bible—and surely of the Talmud— may be far too self-satisfied and utterly blinded by conceit (however scholarly), and therefore dismiss as archaic, anachronistic, "poorly edited," or childish, the significance of all the many so very obvious instances of twos (creations, Adams, Eves, brothers, wives, animals, tablets, etc.) so carefully preserved in the oneness of the Bible. Not merely in the remarkable subtlety, astuteness and fruitfulness of their exegeses, but in the fundamental and challenging moral truths they promulgate, Levinas's Talmudic readings awaken us from the slumber and pretense of tiresome "academic" readings whose alleged openmindedness, forever taking refuge in hypotheses, conjectures, possibilities, however slimly based— though never chosen—is in truth but a more sophisticated form of closemindedness. Closed to self-implication, to responsibility. But humanity has always already been elected to an even greater sobriety than natural being, to be sure, but also greater than that which seems to suffice critical intelligence in the impregnable citadels and sophisticated groves of its "academic" retreats. That scholarship is admirable and worthy, Levinas would be the last to deny, nor would I. But at the same time scholarship is insufficient, inadequate for a fully human life, not only the life of the mind but life among people. Levinas would be the first to affirm this.

The lesson of the two tablets: divinity as absolute mastery reduces humanity to absolute slavery, to subhumanity, to antihumanism. Tablets divine all too divine would have too much authority, would fall to the ground unheeded, would not command *humans*, would belittle humanity, take away dignity, freedom, produce humans less than human, helpless children, groveling supplicants. Such was the slavery in Egypt, naturally aligned with an escapist death cult and a sorcerer's religion. From such slavery the Jews fled, in a negative moment whose positively lay in God's command, under the leadership of Moses and Aaron, a people fleeing with their feet and not only with mouths that prayed, continually moving from slavery, yes, but also toward and up the harder road of freedom, a permanent exodus but also a continual redemption, the very movement of a humanist vision of history. Tablets human all too human, on the other hand, would lack authority, would not *command* humans, would be commanded by humans, by instinct and will to power. Such is the "bad" humanism of the Tower of Babel, of Korach's rebellion, of the Golden Calf, the viperous self-serving rhetoric decried by Heidegger, fundamentalism, and the religious traditions.

Biblical humanism, in contrast, requires the meeting of divine and human through moral command manifest in moral action, hence in human courts, divine command through human response, human response as divinely commanded, absence and presence, preoriginality and originality. No doubt paradoxes abound in such a configuration. No doubt both rationalism and irrationalism chaff under its greater vigilance. Such, however, is the difficult path of a fully human life, the life of the creature, alert in moral exigencies, in the solicitous sobriety of civilized life, attentive to others, charged with obligations and responsibilities, not at all confined to the mind alone, to intellect "intellecting," and, it goes without saying, far more demanding than the impulsive vitality of nature. Rationalism and irrationalism alike would rather be left alone, would rather stay less sober, absorbed in their own affairs, mad or maddening, clever or dumb. The exegetical path, in contrast, requires a more extreme vigilance, an unremitting attention to the ethical alterity of the other.

PHILOSOPHY, RELIGION AND MYTH (CONTRA SPINOZA)

Levinas's Talmudic readings are dedicated to a sober vigilance, to an attentiveness to and for the other, to a moral conscience and conscientiousness; his readings demonstrate the intimate link that binds exegesis, humanism and religion. To see this, it is important to see that exegesis and the stories whose meanings it elaborates must not be confused with myth. "Jewish humanism," Levinas has written elsewhere, is "a system of principles and disciplines that free human life from the prestige of myths, the discord they introduce into ideas and the cruelty they perpetuate in social customs."[5] The enemy of Judaism, and the enemy of all ethical monotheism, then, would be myth, mythological thinking, mythologized life. This is similar to Kant's opposition to "speculative" metaphysics, whose reifications and personifications confuse a regulative ideality with truth claims regarding reality. For Levinas, a truly adult religion offers an alternative perspective attentive, as we have seen, to the transcendent through morality and justice. Concomitant with the moral consciousness of this attentiveness is the effort to rid

---

[5] "For a Jewish Humanism," in Emmanuel Levinas, *Difficult Freedom*, trans. Sean Hand (Baltimore: Johns Hopkins University Press, 1990), 273.

the world of the violence that follows so naturally from the irresponsibility confirmed and sustained by adherence to mythic constructions. Derrida has accused Levinas's critique of philosophy of "violence," but the true violence comes not from an ethical heightening of philosophical awareness, whose transcendence Levinas rightly characterizes as "pacific," but rather from "the prestige of myths, the discord they introduce into ideas and the cruelty they perpetuate in social customs." Levinas is perfectly explicit about the double imperative—positive and negative—which gives sense to the various activities and beliefs that constitute Jewish life: "They held a man freed from myths and identify spirit with justice."[6] In a single but doubled edged exigency, religion would be a movement toward freedom—a difficult freedom, an engaged freedom, to be sure—at the same time that it is a movement away from the violence perpetrated in the name of mythic constructions.

It is instructive to compare Levina's opposition to myth to Spinoza's. Though Spinoza also opposed what he called "superstitious religion," Levinas insists that his own thought remains "at the antipodes of Spinozism."[7] Spinoza's solution to the problem of superstition, and the fear upon which it is based as well as the violence it promotes, is to reject religion altogether in the name of physico-mathematical rationality. Because he feels true freedom can only be found in scientific knowledge, Spinoza identifies all religious constructions, indeed all alternative constructions, with bondage. Levinas, too, as we have seen, opposes myth, and in doing so also opposes superstition. But his opposition, in contrast to Spinoza's,

---

[6] *Difficult Freedom*, 276.
[7] *Totality and Infinity*, 105.

does not repudiate religious transcendence. "Judaism," Levinas has written, "appeals to a humanity devoid of myths—not because the marvelous is repugnant to its narrow soul but because myth, albeit sublime, introduces into the soul that troubled element, that impure element of magic and sorcery and that drunkenness of the Sacred and war, that prolong the animal within the civilized."[8] Both Spinoza and Levinas oppose prolonging "the animal within the civilized," but Spinoza's solution, science all the way down, would throw out the baby with the bathwater. Judaism, for Levinas, is also a force to rid the world of the macabre hybrid demi-gods of Egypt, which are to give way to the one God—the One God of Israel, of all humanity. His solution requires awakening myth not from ignorance in the name of knowledge, as if myth were only ignorance, only a stammering science, which it is not, but rather from its indolence in the name of the more sober and shattering religious responsibilities of a moral and just humanity.

But, one might retort, are not the Bible itself, its stories of Noah's ark, the tablets, the golden calf, the earth swallowing rebels, and the like, as well as the Midrash, and especially the Aggadah upon which Levinas comments in these essays, which are so vital to Judaism, are they not vast compilations of myth? Are they not stories wherein the divine and human are depicted as interacting often in miraculous ways? And if this is so, and so it seems, how can one hope to eradicate myth by means of myth? But the question reveals an unexamined and prejudicial leveling of perspectives. Levinas does not fight myth with myth; rather, he understands the human by means of exegesis. It is a great difference.[9]

---

[8] "Being a Westerner," in Levinas, *Difficult Freedom*, 49.
[9] This same difference, centuries earlier, explains why Spinoza,

Levinas is not satisfied with a radical separation between philosophy and religion. "There is," he writes, "communication between faith and philosophy and not the notorious conflict. Communication in both directions."[10]—The refusal to begin with an irreparable dualism—the refusal to separate reason and revelation, Athens and Jerusalem, philosophy and religion, is one of the great strengths of Levinas's thought. It extends and amplifies, let us note too, a long tradition of Jewish thought and action. The issue is obviously of great importance. In contrast to many philosophers and religious thinkers before him, Levinas overcomes the alleged opposition between science and religion by siding with neither pole. Rather he shifts grounds and undercuts the intellectual temptations of this opposition by writing from a perspective whose unitary vantage point reveals the abstract and derivative character of either side taken independently of the other. If Levinas is "postmodern"—a label both fashionable and deplorable for its slackness, its slickness, its lack of purchase— it is not through any semiotic or semantic pyrotechnics, not through some clever intellectual maneuver, but rather and precisely because his thought challenges the separation of science and religion. And at the same time, he challenges, from an ethical perspective, the plethora of alternative challengers who opt for an aesthetic perspective instead.

One of the claims central to modernity, perhaps even constitutive of modernity, has been the hegemonization of physico-mathematical science. We have heard it since Descartes: only

---

who treated the Bible as myth (or for the ignorant as a very simple-minded moral primer), was so frustrated and infuriated by Maimonides, who despite an intellectual bent no less scientific than Spinoza's, read the Bible in the light of exegesis.

[10] "On Jewish Philosophy," in Emmanuel Levinas, *In the Time of the Nations*, trans. Michael B. Smith (Bloomington: Indiana University Press, 1994), 170.

"clear and distinct" ideas, clear and distinct to the mind, count as accounts of the real. The rest would be subjective, not only opinion and poetry (*poesis*), but ethics and politics, too (this is surely the position of Spinoza, de Sade, and Nietzsche, another set of odd bedfellows). Heidegger and Derrida have denounced this truncation of wisdom, limiting the real to conformity with "clear and distinct ideas," as an unwarranted privileging of presence. Against its domination they have opted for the entertaining but essentially labyrinthean path of an aesthetic-poetic alternative, Heidegger turning to a refined appreciation for vague pre-Socratic fragments and German poets, and Derrida, his most faithful disciple, to microscopic but essentially parasitic analyses of semantic equivocations in texts. There is no doubt that equivocations can always be found, just as the pre-Socratics and poets—as Socrates already showed—can be made to speak many things. But the temporary solace of these clever meanderings, when taken with the utmost seriousness (Heidegger) or with the utmost derision (Derrida), comes at the price of neglecting the prior and more important demands of ethics. Heidegger intones that "thinking is thanking," to which Levinas retorts: "Who is thankful for Auschwitz?" Derrida speaks, finally, of the other and of responsibilities, but in his delicate hands these are no more than texts to be warily deconstructed. These characterizations and the criticism underlying them may strike the reader as harsh, but the political consequences of an unchecked aesthetic worldview have, in fact, been far harsher. Levinas challenges the hegemony of epistemology and its concomitant truncation of reason by means of an ethical metaphysics—that is to say, by means of an ethical account of transcendence that exceeds but at the same time requires knowledge. For reason to be reasonable it must neither be rational alone, nor absorbed by its irreducible poetic-rhetorical dimension; it must rather be responsible.[11]

In the face of modern nonteleological science, the temptation to simply separate religion and philosophy is great. A thinker of modernity as clearheaded, self-conscious and insightful as Leo Strauss develops many reasons to defend an irreconcilable conflict between religion and philosophy, Athens and Jerusalem, reason and revelation. But, so it seems to me, he has nonetheless, for all his clarity, succumbed to a pervasive but unacknowledged Spinozist presupposition underlying such a separation. It was Spinoza, after all, who in the *Theologico-Political Treatise* explicitly, trenchantly and systematically separated reason from revelation, differentiating them in terms of rational truth and irrational belief, knowledge and ignorance, freedom and bondage. Spinoza, like Strauss, Levinas and a long philosophical tradtion, rightfully wanted to oppose and eradicate a superstitious mythological type of religion. Against the fearful and potentially fearsome prejudices and the loss of human dignity that follows from submission to superstition, all three thinkers argue instead for a spiritually purified or "adult" conception of religion. Spinoza's position, however, is determined throughout by an unconditional acceptance of the modern physico-mathematical model of rationality and science. This was, in

---

[11] One thinks of Kierkegaard's distinction: "Aesthetic pathos keeps itself at a distance from existence, or is in existence in a state of illusion; while existential pathos dedicates itself more and more profoundly to the task of existing, and with the consciousness of what existence is, penetrates all illusions, becoming more and more concrete through reconstructing existence in action." Sören Kierkeggard, *Concluding Unscientific Postscript*, trans. David F. Swenson and Walter Lowrie (Princeton: Princeton University Press: 1941), 387.

fact, the basis of Spinoza's critique of Descartes: Descartes was not modern enough, did not fully carry out his own commitment to mathematical truth, to clear and distinct ideas.

Spinoza argues that not only mythology, but imagination *per se* is altogether incompetent to conceive the clear and distinct ideas which are to be the exclusive domain of genuine science. Spinoza's *Ethics* intends to be nothing other, and nothing less, than the self-understanding of science conceived as the only and complete system of truth. It aims to eradicate "knowledge of the first kind"[12]—which is to say, imagination, opinion, false ideas (everything Spinoza finds in the Bible)—for the sake of the fully coherent and progressively more determinate system of necessary and universal propositions (of material causality and deductive logic) which make up "knowledge of the second kind"—scientific or fully rational knowledge. The *Ethics* is intended to be "the way of truth," to borrow Parmenides' phrase, in contrast to imagination and opinion, which Spinoza derides as "knowledge of the first kind." Science is possible when the mind frees itself from the pernicious influence of the imagination. By means of a mathematical standard, Spinoza completes the attack on myth and *poesis* begun by Parmenides, banishing them, as Plato and not been able, from the precincts of truth. Only the pure self-transparency opened by mathematical clarity and distinctness, yielding universal and necessary truth, as opposed to the impenetrable opacity and heteronomy of

---

[12] Baruch Spinoza, *Ethics*, trans. Samuel Shirley (Indianapolis: Hackett Publishing Co., 1992), Part II, Scholium 2 to Proposition 40, and Proposition 41 (90–91). Spinoza explicitly equates "knowledge of the first kind" with "'opinion' or 'imagination'" (Part II, Scholium 2 to Proposition 40; 90), and declares in Proposition 41 that: "Knowledge of the first kind is the only cause of falsity" (91).

mythic tales and all products of the imagination (which leave humanity vulnerable and obedient to the external forces Levinas calls "magic and sorcery and that drunkenness of the Sacred and war") would be adequate to a fully free and hence fully human spirituality. Such is Spinoza's rigorous program of science qua ethics. Its price is the belittlement and its aim is the ultimate elimination of religion.

For Spinoza, religion and theology would be based in ignorance, untruth and heteronomy, and would always already be a politics. Hence the hyphenated title of Spinoza's treatise on religion, *Theologico-Political Treatise*, a book that does not simply treat religion and politics at the same time, but must treat them together because it reduces religion to a politics, to force relations, to the manipulation of meanings rather than the discovery of truth. In chapter seven of the *Theologico-Political Treatise*, entitled "On the Interpretation of Scriptures," Spinoza declares that "the point at issue is *merely* [my italics] the meaning of the texts, not their truth."[13] His point, and the central aim of the entire *Theologico-Political Treatise*, is to sharply distinguish truth from meaning, rationality from theology, in no way hiding his scorn for the ruses of religion and theology and their imaginary productions, despite their usefulness—given the ignorance of the "masses," the "multitude"—for a prudential political calculation. Thus Spinoza extends on the deepest philosophical plane, in the name of science, the divorce of fact and value that Machiavelli had earlier encouraged on the plane of political calculation. Science, philosophy, freedom, and calculation for the intellectual few; the Bible, religion, obedience, and

---

[13] Baruch Spinoza, *Tractatus Theologico-Politicus*, trans. Samuel Shirley (Leiden: E.J. Brill, 1991), 143.

ignorance for the many. Nietzsche will later admire this seg-
regation of the few from the many, while shifting his criteria
from knowledge and ignorance to strength and weakness.

It is true that a thinker such as Strauss, unlike Spinoza,
will recognize the independence and perhaps even the superiority of monotheism over mythology. Unlike Spinoza, too,
Strauss will argue that the rights of monotheistic religion
are impregnable against philosophical criticism, that philosophy is as helpless to refute religion as religion is to refute
philosophy. Nonetheless, despite Strauss's differences from
Spinoza, his position remains unwittingly based on Spinozist
premises, on a sharp and irreconcilable separation of the
truths of philosophy from the claims, however unitary, of
religion. Levinas, in contrast, rejects this dichotomy, rejects
its Spinozist philosophical presuppositions. The plurality of
myths poses the problem of contradiction and conflict, to be
sure. But this problem is fatal only on the assumption that
scientific philosophy has the last word. The genuine resolu-
tion to this problem, and to the alleged conflict of reason and
revelation, lies neither in philosophy nor religion taken separately. Reason and imagination—or, more broadly, reason and
sensibility—while not reducible to one another, are at the
same time indispensable to one another. Or, to restate this
alleged opposition in terms of reason and will, the solution
lies neither in reason without will—i.e., will reduced to reason—nor in will without reason—i.e., blind and stupid faith.
Levinas's Talmudic readings demonstrate and rise to another
way, a more exacting intersection of reason and religion across
exegesis, and across exegesis they rise to ethics.

CRITICISM AND THE LIFE OF EXEGESIS

The solution to the problem of myths contradicting myths
lies neither in the abstract transparency of an allegedly pure

reason, which eliminates imagination and free will along with myth, nor in the no less abstract and complementary opacity of blind faith, which denies free will and intellect. These alleged solutions represent two sides of the same coin, a coin that separates reason from revelation. Neither does the solution lie in embracing myth as if on a higher plane, relying on the words and visions of great poets or obscure fragments, seducing a frustrated philosophical reason with a self-referring groundlessness. Such a path, for all its refinement, remains a complacency, and at bottom another version of blind faith, defenseless against moral and political manipulation. Rather, the solution lies in recognizing the deeper link between reason and faith in exegesis. Exegesis, Levinas writes, effects "a demythologizing of the text"[14] for the sake of a "wisdom of love"; it is indeed the very performance, manifestation, production of a wisdom that serves the ends of morality and justice: "*a difficult wisdom concerned with truths that correlate to virtues.*"[15]

As in all the humanities, understanding in religion is, of course, to the highest degree self-understanding. Hence it is dependent on hermeneutics, or interpretation, because the object of human understanding here, in contrast to the object of explanation in the natural sciences, is the very same humanity that is the subject of human understanding. Religion is, in a word, self-understanding. In contrast, however, to the self-understanding obtained through literature or historical studies, religion is humanity's self-understanding in

---

[14] "On Jewish Philosophy," Levinas, *In the Time of the Nations*, 168.
[15] "For a Jewish Humanism," Levinas, *Difficult Freedom*, 275, my italics.

view of the absolute transcendence of God. To grasp the import of Levinas's philosophical contribution, his "solution" to the alleged opposition between science and religion, and the problem of myths conflicting with myths, we must make a distinction between two modes of interpretation. These two modes of interpretation can be taken narrowly as two types of text interpretation or more broadly as two different existential stances toward truth and meaning. One is *criticism* and the other *exegesis*, of which Talmudic exegesis is for Levinas the exemplary case.

What criticism does is to interpret a text by explaining it in terms of more or less remote objective contexts. One understands the biblical flood story, for example, by comparing it, say, to a contemporaneous Mesopotamian flood story, or to our current scientific knowledge regarding floods. One understands Abraham's childhood, his opposition to idolatry, and his early departure from his hometown, by grasping the economic, social, and political contexts inferred from archeological digs in the ancient city of Ur in present day Iraq. The key to criticism, then, is explanation by comparison and contrast derived from a text's insertion within local, regional, and ultimately global contexts, e.g., meteorological, geological, geographical, historical, cultural, economic, political, religious, sociological, and linguistic contexts. One locates a text within a universal and objective differential field of texts and contexts.

Exegesis, on the other hand, is text interpretation not through *explanation* derived from *objective* context alone, but through *understanding* derived from the text's as well as the subject's own *subjective* context. Though it does not exclude objective truth, for this too is also part of subjective context, it searches for subjective or internal truth as well. The term "subjective," borrowed from modern epistemology, may be misleading. Rather than restricting the explanation of a text's meaning to significations derived by comparing and contrasting its formal or structural characteristics with those of alternative cultures, exegesis would understand the significance of a text by comparing and contrasting its content or intent with those from that text's own cultural tradition or from cultural traditions internally relevant to the text, *and* to cultural traditions that ultimately refer to the cultural context of the interpreter. One might call exegesis "relevant hermeneutics," regardless of how objectively remote the texts may be from the inquirer's own cultural-spiritual tradition. And the import of "relevance"—text as teaching—is irreducible because the inquirer and the text are bound, more or less remotely, within the all-embracing but infinite context of one humanity—humanism again. Exegesis, then, is part and parcel of the internal and ongoing self-revelatory dimension of a living textual tradition, while criticism contributes to the external and objective knowledge of a universal science for which any particular text is but one text among others. "But the lucid labors of that science," Levinas notes of the latter, "have never been able, to this day, to take the place of that other reading, which is neither the private domain of the so-called 'orthodox' circles, not the stylized daily practice of the underdeveloped classes."[16] "[E]xegesis," Levinas writes, "made the text speak; while critical philology speaks *of* this text. The one takes the text to be a source of teaching, the other treats it as a thing."[17] Of course exegesis has no good

---

[16] "The Strings and the Wood," in Emmanuel Levinas, *Outside the Subject*, trans. Michael B. Smith (Stanford: Stanford University Press, 1994), 128.

[17] "The State of Israel and the Religion of Israel," trans. Sean Hand, in *The Levinas Reader*, ed. Sean Hand (Oxford: Basil Blackwell, 1989), 263.

reason to ignore the claims of criticism, but neither can it be limited to or bound to them.

An important point must be highlighted. To distinguish between exegesis and criticism does not imply that the significance of exegesis is any less universal than that of criticism. This must be highlighted because there is considerable prejudice against this claim to universality from the side of those scholarly practitioners who, for one reason or another, limit themselves (or appear to limit themselves) exclusively to criticism. There is no doubt that one of the virtues of criticism is objectivity and the universality that objectivity implies. And, even further, to suggest that criticism is itself a version of exegesis is in no way intended to undermine its objectively. One of the prime virtues of exegesis, in contrast to myth, is also universality, even if it is not based on the same principles of objectivity that the external perspective of criticism provides. Above and beyond, as it were, the objective scientific explanations gained through criticism, and above and beyond an exegesis that might want, according to its own self-interpretation, to contribute only to the internal growth of self-understanding within a particular living tradition (what Levinas has called "the so-called 'orthodox' circles"), exegesis is no less capable of contributing to the self-understanding of humankind at large. It is precisely this point that Levinas—along with his contemporaries Abraham Joshua Heschel and Andre Neher, to name only two colleagues within the Jewish exegetical tradition—will insist upon. He will further show that this is the case, in the third essay of this volume, with rabbinical or Talmudic exegesis, where biblical narratives and stories of the sages and others are taken neither as authoritative myths nor as simpleminded children's tales, but, as we shall see, as exemplary *paradigms*. Exegesis can be, and Talmudic exegesis is, an enlightened discourse, a wisdom, for each and every individual, whether Jewish, Christian, Muslim, Confucian, Hindu, Buddhist, or atheist, to speak only of religious denominations. For precisely this reason, coupled with his understanding of Judaism as permeated by rabbinic exegesis, Levinas calls the heart of Judaism a "Jewish humanism" or a "biblical humanism." It is for humanity. "It may even be," he muses rhetorically, knowing the prestige and pride of criticism in today's intellectual circles, "that a less naive conception of the inspired Word than the one expiring beneath critical pens allows the true message to come through."[18]

With the above distinction in mind, we are in a position to clarify the central role of exegesis in Levinas's conception of religion. His claim is, first of all, that Jewish spirituality is exegetical through and through. Just as Judaism cannot be separated from Torah, Torah cannot be separated from exegesis. One does not simply read the Bible through the Talmud, say, as if the Talmud were a gloss that could be stripped off; there is no pure Bible, but only a Bible interpreted, and there is a specifically "Jewish" Bible precisely owing to the Talmud. Second, the exegesis that cannot be separated from Torah is a wisdom that combines understanding and virtue. This is what Spinoza failed to appreciate. Third, precisely because it eliminates the mythological, and because it aims at virtue, it is a contribution to universal self-understanding. Levinas thus rejects the adequacy of both the rhetoric of an ostensive literalism as found in fundamentalist readings, which he will call "the negation of the spiritual and the source of all idolatry,"[19] and the rhetoric of a ostensive detachment derived from a strictly scientific or critical reading. The

---

[18] "The Strings and the Wood," Levinas, *Outside the Subject*, 126.
[19] "Contempt for the Torah as Idolatry," Levinas, *In the Time of the Nations*, 67.

rhetoric of both these approaches, one in the name of whole-hearted conviction, the other in the name of openminded dis-engagement, are narrow forms of reading alien to the integral combination of multiple readers and multiple levels of mean-ing, and the prescriptive heights uncovered and unraveled by means of exegesis.

Levinas writes often of the peculiar genius of Talmudic exegesis, at once particular and universal, faithful to the concrete situations of humanity yet resonating with trans-temporal significance. The significance of such a reading is universal not because it abstractly applies to everyone in gen-eral, as, for example, does the period table of chemisty, but rather because it concretely speaks to each and every indi-vidual in particular in his or her particularity. For Levinas, as I have indicated, Judaism is permeated throughout by exegesis, and owing to this immersion in reading and rereading, it avoids the moribund idolatries of literalism and scientism. In an article entitled "Contempt for the Torah as Idolatry," Levinas writes of the compulsory and mutual char-acter of the exegetical interaction between reading and read as follows:

> I wish to speak of the Torah as desirous of being a force ward-ing off idolatry by its essence as Book, that is, by its very writing, signifying precisely prescription and by the perma-nent reading it calls for—permanent reading or interpreta-tion and reinterpretation or study; a book thus destined from the start for its Talmudic life. A book that is also by that very fact foreign to any blind commitment . . . The reading or study of a text that protects itself from the eventual idolatry of this very text, by renewing, through continual exegesis—and ex-egesis of that exegesis—the immutable letters and hearing the breath of the living God in them . . . Reading and study taking on a liturgical meaning in Jewish culture: that of an

entering . . . into society, into a covenant with the transcendent
will . . . A liturgy of study as lofty as obedience to the precepts, but of a never-ending study, for one is never done with
the other. Incompleteness that is the law of love: it is the future itself, the coming of a world that never ceases coming,
but also the excellence of that coming compared to presence
as persistence in being and in what has always been.[20]

Levinas is thus able to reject the narrow literalism of a blind
faith, without, however, thereby rejecting the personalism,
the existential rebound, and the fervor of its commitment.
In the same way, he is able to reject the free-floating abstractness, the alleged "superiority" of criticism—which Rosenzweig
had earlier decried as mere free-floating "possibility," the
possible divorced from the actual, leading not to life but to a
"phantom"[21] life—without thereby rejecting universality.

In contrast to blind faith or detached criticism, exegesis
produces and requires the engaged or existential self-transformation of the inquirer, through a back-and-forth movement, the very life of inquiry as dialogue between text and
reader,[22] between reader and reader, between texts, readers
and reality across time, from an immemorial past to an ever
distant future. "[T]he life of a Talmudist is nothing but the

---

[20] Ibid., 58–59.

[21] *Franz Rosenzweig: His Life and Thought*, ed. Nahum N. Glatzer
(New York: Schocken Books, 1967), 97, 129. For more on Rosenzweig's rejection of the abstractness of scientific knowledge, see my
article, "Rosenzweig's Rebbe Halevi: From the Academy to the Yeshiva," in *Judaism*, issue no. 176, vol. 44, no. 4 (Fall 1995): 448–66.

[22] Basing himself on Buber rather than Levinas, Steven Kepnes
will propose precisely such a model of reading in Part I of his book,
*The Text as Thou: Martin Buber's Dialogical Hermeneutics and
Narrative Theology* (Bloomington: Indiana University Press, 1992),
3–78.

permanent renewal of the letter through the intelligence."[23] For Levinas this manner of exegetical reading results in "saving the text from being turned into a mere book, that is to say just a thing, and in once more allowing it to resonate with the great and living voice of teaching."[24]

FOUR CHARACTERISTICS OF EXEGESIS (CONTRA NIETZSCHE)

One can distinguish in exegesis four interrelated characteristics or dimensions: (1) productive integrity of spirit and letter, (2) pluralism of persons and readings, (3) existential or self-transformative wisdom, and (4) renewal of a living ethico-religious tradition.[25] It is interesting to note, given the academic popularity of Nietzsche and his epigones, that exegesis resembles in its first three characteristics Nietzsche's conception of interpretation. Regarding the fourth point, however, Levinas and Nietzsche radically part company, as Nietzsche attacks the very ethico-religious tradition that Levinas defends and renews. The chasm that separates the outcomes of their respective perspectives measures the importance of the fourth dimension of exegesis—continuity with a living ethico-religious tradition—and serves to explain, as

---

[23] "As Old as the World," Levinas, *Nine Talmudic Readings*, 79.

[24] Levinas, "The State of Israel and the Religion of Israel," *The Levinas Reader*, 263.

[25] It should be noted from the start that Levinas's "interpretation" of rabbinic exegesis is in nowise ideosyncratic, wishful thinking, or invented. For a very fine account along the same lines of the living and authoritative dialectic operative in rabbinic exegesis—called "Intrinsic Inspiration" (lxv)—in contrast to both strict literalism and loose liberalism, see Howard Loewe's 1938 "Introduction" to *A Rabbinic Anthology*, ed. C.G. Montefiore & H. Loewe (New York: Schocken Books, 1974), especially lv–lxxxi.

I shall note later, why Levinas and Nietzsche only *seem* to agree regarding the first three characteristics. I turn now to a closer look at these four characteristic of exegesis.

(1) Productive integrity of spirit and letter. Following and developing the phenomenological insights of Henri Bergson and Merleau-Ponty, Levinas begins with the integral or dialectical unity of spirit and matter. At the level of text interpretation, this translates into the integral unity of spirit and letter, meaning and text. Letters give rise to spirit, call for commentary,[26] and spirit is rooted in letters, in a textual richness that is one of the marks of sacred literature, or of literature taken in a sacred sense. Beginning with this integrity, exegesis succumbs neither to an impossible literalism of the letter, which Levinas derides as the "negation of all spirituality and the source of all idolatry,"[27] nor to a no less impossible detachment, an abstract or free-floating interpretation, which Levinas derides as "pious rhetoric . . . in which ambiguity, amidst unverifiable 'mysteries,' always find a convenient shelter."[28] Literalism and spiritualism are both subjective in the worst sense: willful, unregulated, self-projections, rather than inspirations. Spirit detached from the letter—one might think of certain instances of Protestant Bible reading in America (as well as of Derrida)—gives rise to an excessive

---

[26] In *Sotah* 47b, the Torah is said to "beg from house to house to house" in order to get students. Cited in *A Rabbinic Anthology*, ed. C.G. Montefiore & H. Loewe, 668.

[27] In the Talmud we find the following remarkable declaration: "Jerusalem was destroyed only because they gave judgment therein literally in accordance with biblical law (Baba Metzia, 30b).

[28] Levinas, "Contempt for the Torah as Idolatry," *In the Time of the Nations*, 63.

and hence a falsely optimistic moralistic generosity,[29] to an "angelic" dreaminess inattentive and unattached to the historical situations and concrete motives of the human condition. By contrast, in exegesis, "through the apparent attachment to the letter, there is the extreme attention paid to the spirit of the biblical text and a hermeneutic which puts a passage . . . back into the context of the totality of the Bible, with a view to deepening."[30] To fly with a text, to be inspired by it and discover its inspiration, requires not that one have wings, that one hover above it. Rather, it is with one's feet firmly planted on the earth—with a properly human dignity—that one is able to find the wings of words that cry out to rise to their proper height and raise the reader to his or her proper height as well.

(2) Pluralism of persons and readings. Exegesis not only yields but requires multiple readings and interpretations. This multiplicity, however, is not a flaw, as has all too often been asserted—happily or unhappily—based on the standard of an epistemological rigidity satisfied only in mathematics (and not even there). Rather, it is a product of and tribute to the pluralism constitutive of human society, and to the ethics such pluralism bears, on the one hand, as it is also a

---

[29] "The Pact," Levinas, *Beyond the Verse*, 78–79: "A principle of generosity, but nothing but a principle. . . . Every generous thought is threatened by its Stalinism. The great strength of the Talmud's casuistry is to be the special discipline which seeks in the particular the precise moment at which the general principle runs the danger of becoming its own contrary, and watches over the general in the light of the particular."

[30] "On Religious Language and the Fear of God," in Emmanuel Levinas, *Beyond the Verse*, trans. Gary Mole (Bloomington: Indiana University Press, 1994), 91.

product of and tribute to the essential pluralism (not "mere" or "unfortunate" ambiguity or equivocation) of textual meaning, on the other. "Each one of us Jews," Levinas once declared before presenting a public interpretation of Judaism, and without any false modesty, "retains his freedom of expression."[31] This qualification could well serve as a preface to all of Levinas's Talmudic readings, as indeed to all reading and communication. Regardless of the depth and sincerity of one's own religious commitments, no reader can appropriate the definitive mantle or chant of priest or pontiff (and even less of oracle), because the revelatory character of Judaism as a living exegetical tradition cannot sanction an official dogma or catechism. Without opening itself to any and all interpretations, the Midrash insists that millions of interpretations of the Torah, more even for non-Jews than for Jews, were already given and hence legitimated at Sinai.[32] In Levinas's vocabulary this also means that each human being retains his or her freedom of expression because that expression is not extraneous to truth, is not a merely subjective interference, or the source of merely secondary qualities. Rather, expression, commentary, dialogue, partnership in learning, are the necessary "manner" or "way" of truth

---

[31] Levinas, "Judaism and Christianity," *In the Time of the Nations*, 161.

[32] According to Midrash the Torah at Sinai was given to 600,000 souls, for each of whom it was received differently; and it was given with at least four ways of interpretation ("PaRDeS": literal, allegorical, homelitic, mystical), yielding 2,400,000 readings; and it was given even then to the seventy nations, yielding 170,400,000 readings; all of which is to say that the there are innumerable legitimate readings, each necessary for a complete understanding of Torah; which is to say that Torah is inexhaustible.

itself, since truth cannot be true without reflecting rather than suppressing its actual conditions.

"Prophecy," Levinas will say elsewhere, using this term in a broad sense, "is an essential dimension of truth."[33] This does not reduce truth to subjectivity, or diminish truth in the name of friendship, say—or it need not, because truth itself, for its full expression as a living ongoing revelation, requires multiple expressions. Speaking of revelation and the multiplicity of legitimate readings, Levinas writes:

> The Revelation has a particular way of producing meaning, which lies in its calling upon the unique within me. It is as if a multiplicity of persons . . . as if each person, by virtue of his own uniqueness, were able to guarantee the revelation of one unique aspect of the truth, so that some of its facets would never have been revealed if certain people had been absent from mankind . . . I am suggesting that the totality of truth is made out of the contributions of a multiplicity of people: the uniqueness of each act of listening carries the secret of the text; the voice of Revelation, in precisely the inflection lent by each persons's ear, is necessary for the truth of the Whole. . . . The multiplicity of people, each one of them indispensable, is necessary to produce all the dimensions of meaning; the multiplicity of meanings is due to the multiplicity of people.[34]

Like Schleiermacher in this regard,[35] Levinas will argue that there are, in principle, at least as many readings as readers. Each reader brings (or can bring) his or her own unique

---

[33] Compare with Numbers 21.29: "Moses said to him [Joshua son of Nun], "Are you being zealous for my sake? Would that the entire people of God could be prophets."

[34] Levinas, "Revelation in Jewish Tradition," *The Levinas Reader*, 195.

[35] "We all exist as 'someone.' Therefore each person has a greater receptivity for some religious perceptions and feelings than for

concerns, insights, perspectives, and heritage to bear in understanding what a text can say, and what a text can say depends on this multiplicity of readers and readings.

Thus in the revelation proper to religion "there is included a semantics that is absolute, inexhaustible, ever renewable through exegesis."[36] This inexhaustible pluralism and the diversity to which it gives rise is not a *flaw* or *problem*, but rather a reflection of the irreducible alterity and personal challenge encountered in social relations. Of the "innumerable" exegetical interpretations, Levinas writes: "Their diversity, their very contradictions, far from compromising the truths commented upon, are felt to be faithful to the Real, refractory to the System."[37] Revelation thus extends through the pluralism of persons[38] and readings throughout history right up to the present, as Levinas notes, recalling the celebrated insight of an eighteenth century rabbi for whom "the slightest question put to the schoolmaster by a novice constitutes an ineluctable articulation of the Revelation which was heard at Sinai."[39] Pluralism and diversity, however, are

---

others. In this manner every person's experience is different." From F.D.E. Schleiermacher, "Speeches on Religion," in *German Essays on Religion*, ed. Edward Oakes (New York: Continuum, 1994), 56. Levinas, of course, does not reduce unique religious experience to "perceptions and feelings."

[36] "From Ethics to Exegesis," Levinas, *In the Time of the Nations*, 112.

[37] "The Strings and the Wood," Levinas, *Outside the Subject*, 130.

[38] In *Ta'an*, 7a: "A Rabbi said that as fire does not burn when isolated, so will the words of the Torah not be preserved when studied by oneself alone. Another said that the learned who are occupied in the study of the Law, each one by himself, deserve punishment, and they shall become fools." Cited in *A Rabbinic Anthology*, 107.

[39] "Revelation in Jewish Tradition," Levinas, *The Levinas Reader*, 195.

not equivalent to fragmentation; we shall return shortly to consider the unity that brings even apparently contradictory truths together across a long history.

(3) Wisdom or existential self-transformation. This third characteristic of exegesis is closely related to the second. The dialectical or dialogical manifestation of exegesis is not merely a spectacle, seen at a distance in the third person; rather, it transforms and is meant to transform its interlocutors in the first person. "I" and "you" (including the "you" which speaks through the text),[40] are thus not the same as "one" and "it," or the same as "self" and "other person." Exegesis lives because it engages the lives of those who engage in it. This is why "Talmud Torah," the study of sacred literature, which includes a vast range of literature, is in the Jewish tradition called "learning" (Yiddish: *lernen*). This is also why the Yiddish term for synagogue, "*shul*," literally means "school." The significance of a text—inseparable from exegesis—is neither a subjective projection, as if the self remained inviolable and imposed itself on the text, nor an impossible literalism, as if the self again remained the same but discovered something outside itself, unmoved and unmovable in the text. Rather, significance is itself an existential enterprise, fraught

---

[40] It is interesting in this regard that in orthodox yeshivah exegetical circles sometimes a revered sage-author becomes known and (re)named by the title of his primary book (e.g., Rabbi Yisroel Meir HaCohen Kagan (1838–1933) is known after his book as "Ha-*Chofetz Chaim*," (The "Will to Life"), Rabbi Meir Simcha HaCohen (1834–1923) is known as "Ha-*Or Someyach*" (The "Joyful Light")); and very often important religious books (*Midrash, Talmud,* commentaries, codes) are spoken of as if they were live personages, e.g., "The *Midrash* says . . .," or "The *Mishnah Torah* says . . ." rather than "Maimonides says. . . ."

with difficulties and dangers, but also rewards. It is an existential enterprise, an intertwining of inwardness and exteriority that emerges in and affects the interaction which is exegetical reading. Written Torah cannot be separated from Oral Torah without becoming "dry bones," just as Oral Torah cannot be separated from Written Torah without producing "beautiful souls," both of which are abstractions alien to the readers and writings they claim to elucidate.

One does not walk away from learning, or engage in it, with a new or revised set of theses in one's pocket; rather, one is changed by the experience of learning. Thus the Talmud enjoins Talmudic study even for those poor students whose retain nothing afterwards! Learning in Judaism is itself a quasi-liturgical activity. In contrast to criticism that may alter an objective body of knowledge, in exegetical reading—even of the most obscure and seemingly impractical texts, texts, say, that refer to rituals and practices that have not been performed for thousands of years—the reader is in principle still changed, transformed, uplifted, inspired by the reading. In learning, one's aim is never simply to put a learned idea into practice: the learning is also practice. Indicative of this approach, it is often the case that after hours of intense Talmudic study, requiring great intelligence, diligence, as well as keen logical and analytical skills to decipher and understand a text, students may conclude their learning by asking: "And what do we [as observant Jews] actually do?" and then look up the answer elsewhere in a contemporary code book. The Talmud is called an "ocean," indicating its vastness. But the image further suggests that, as in entering an ocean, the student gets wet, develops muscles, and must swim for dear life—Talmudic study is a complete spiritual-intellectual immersion.

Exegesis cannot be action at a distance or pure intellection, but it must be an existential project because it contains an ineradicable *prescriptive* dimension. One does not learn about Temple ceremonies, say, in order to perform them; no one is oblivious to the fact that the Temple no longer stands. Rather, in learning about Temple rituals, one also learns about one's relation to God, to others, the meaning of priesthood, sacrifice, holiness, purity, etc. Perhaps, too—and this level of meaning is never lost—one day the obsolete ceremonies *will* be performed. Who knows? nothing can be discounted in the wealth of sacred meaning. There are levels and levels of significance. Also, it should not be forgotten, very often learning does have to do with practices and beliefs that are still current, and thus enriches them with new layers of significance. It was "study," Levinas writes, "that was considered valid as *association*, as covenant, as sociality with God—with his will, which, though not incarnate, is inscribed in the Torah."[41] Exegesis thus tolerates neither detached knowledge nor blind faith, but promotes wisdom, a way of life, and a way toward a way of life, a combination of truth inextricably bound to behavior and behavior inextricably bound to truth: "a difficult wisdom," as Levinas has said, "concerned with truths that correlate to virtues." It impetus is vertical as well as horizontal, finding the vertical in the horizontal.

Exegetical wisdom is difficult precisely because it operates neither above nor below the human condition, but speaks a *human* language. This language is charged with prescriptive inspiration, with moral commands, duties, obligations, responsibilities. It speaks to readers in their whole being as

---

[41] "Judaism and Kenosis," Levinas, *Difficult Freedom*, 120.

individuals, as family members, as members of communities, polities, and a global humanity, and not merely to intellects or to scholarly interests. Approached in this way, the sacred stories resist devolving into myths. "In opposition to the transfiguration into myth," Levinas write, "(whether by degradation or sublimation) that threatens this 'profound past,' there stands the astonishing reality of today's Jews . . . As a defense against 'mythologizing,' . . . these traits also characterize the liturgy . . . At once commemoration of Sacred History and a continuation of the events commemorated, the practices are, through *interpretation*, reinserted into the texture of those events."[42]

(4) Renewal of a living tradition through paradigmatics. The third characteristic of exegesis, self-transformation, is linked, for Levinas, to the fourth and perhaps most important characteristic of exegesis: connection with a historical and more or less organized ethical tradition. While interpretations are innumerable and inexhaustible, they are nonetheless rooted in past interpretations, in past texts, in texts that have a past, in a past aiming at a future, in a tradition that in the case of Judaism is, in Levinas's words, "as old as the world," that is to say, as old as the "humanity of the human." Certainly this is one of the central (exegetical) truths taught by the dating of the Jewish lunar calendar, nearly 6,000 years old. It tells the story not of the geology of the earth, or of the evolutionary origins of homo sapiens, but rather of the humanity of the human, the origins of *our* universe of meaning.[43] Adam would not be the first home sapien (for who, after all, did Cain go off and marry? a question asked

---

[42] "The Strings and the Wood," Levinas, *Outside the Subject*, 128.
[43] On this point I recommend Leo Strauss's penetrating exegesis

by all third grade Sunday school students), but rather, as his very name ("Adam" = "human") suggests, the first human being—ideality and reality combined. As such, Adam serves as a paradigm: of intimate relations with God, with commandments, with a spouse, with nature, etc. What regulates exegesis, and at the same time frees it from both the excessive rigidity of objectivism and the excessive elasticity of subjectivism, is its living link with tradition.

This fourth characteristic of exegesis, then, is a specification or determination of the third characteristic, the dialectical interaction between texts, readers, history, and transcendence. It refers to specific historical commitments and to the extensions of these commitments, these living interactions, under the guidance and weight of tradition. Levinas is thus able to remind his readers of the all important conjunction of liberty and authority in exegesis:

> There is, moreover, a means of discriminating between personal originality brought to bear upon the reading of the Book and the play of the phantasms of amateurs (or even charlatans): this is provided by the necessity of referring subjective findings to the continuity of readings through history, the tradition of commentaries which no excuse of direct inspiration from the text allows one to ignore. No "renewal" worthy of the name can dispense with these references.[44]

Liberty and revelation are bound by tradition, just as tradition lives through revelation and liberty.

Tradition provides a regulating context for the historical

---

of the biblical genesis story in "On the Interpretation of Genesis," in Strauss, *Jewish Philosophy and the Crisis of Modernity*, ed. Kenneth Hart Green (Albany: SUNY Press, 1997), 359–76.

[44] "Revelation in Jewish Tradition," Levinas, *The Levinas Reader*, 196.

dialectic of a past renewed in the present opening upon and opening up a novel future. Wakened by exegesis, both text and reader are made to link up with and reawaken a long tradition of prior exegesis. Along these same lines, Franz Rosenzweig once wrote, "To read Hebrew implies a readiness to assume the total heritage of the language . . . Its [Hebrew's] growth is not that of an organism but of a treasure."[45] Just as every word of the sacred Hebrew literature resonates with and is linked to every other word of that literature, exactly so does every exegesis resonate with and link up with every other, in principle if not in fact. "To belong to a book," Levinas writes, "as one belongs to one's history!"[46] By an odd twist, then, what is today often referred to as Jewish "orthodox fundamentalism" is precisely the opposite of Christian Protestant "fundamentalism": the learned Jew opens the Bible to read it through the long historical lens of innumerable commentaries, while the latter opens the Bible and reads afresh as if for the first time. Of course, reading the Bible through commentaries includes reading it afresh for the first time. To read, even for the first time, is to reread, and to reread is to read for the first time. Exegesis is at once old and new, derivative and original—again, "diachrony." "There is nothing new under the sun," wrote Solomon in *Ecclesiastes*, not because everything has been said and done and therefore need not be said or done again, but because everything new renews, and every renewal is a new beginning, a new passing or passage of the past. Thus in the same text Solomon also writes: "The words of the wise are like goads."

---

[45] *Franz Rosenzweig: His Life and Thought*, ed. Nahum N. Glatzer (New York: Schocken Books, 1967), 268, 267.

[46] "The Strings and the Wood," Levinas, *Outside the Subject*, 129.

Exegesis awakens a peculiar time structure: more past than origins, hence "immemorial," yet more future than projection, hence "messianic." Through exegesis, wisdom reaches to the roots and heights of an always ruptured and renewed human continuity. "It is the eternal anteriority of wisdom," Levinas writes, "with respect to science and history."[47] The letters of Jewish tradition solicit interpretation because the reader of sacred texts comes to them from neither dead history nor mystifying mythology, but formed by the very meanings whose meaning must be awakened anew. Reading produces rereading. Exegesis produces its own renewal. Thus for Levinas, the tales, stories, narratives of Bible, Midrash, and Aggadah offer eternal "paradigms." The vivid concretude of the Bible, Midrash and Aggadah, need not turn into fossils, embedded in a long gone stratum, true then but false now, as modern overly hasty reformers and critics have suggested. Rather, the stories remain rich treasure houses of meaning, precisely to the extent that they remain alive through exegesis, that is to say, to the extent that one finds them applicable today. Not, of course, because when the ancient texts speak of donkeys and wooden carts they already had automobiles and trucks in mind, but rather because the human imperatives that speak through these texts lend themselves to and require the continual renewal of exegesis, right from the very start.[48] There is no original word, but no obsolete word either—such is the unity of humankind.

---

[47] "Judaism and the Present," Levinas, *The Levinas Reader*, 257.

[48] The midrashic story of Moses, uncomprehending, sitting in the classroom of Rabbi Akiva, who nonetheless expounds the Torah "in the name of Moses, our teacher," is but one of many indications that the sacred literature is itself aware of its own prolongation through exegesis.

Exegesis is thus not some nefarious manipulation and distortion of revelation, as Spinoza thought because he wanted to bury history and its revelations once and for all in the name of the latest science. Rather, it is a continual animation, a permanent awakening, the very revelation of revelation. It is a mistake to conceive revelation as once and done with, locked into the "once upon a time" of fable. Exegesis, like revelation (the two are inseparable), is once and forever, once again, and again and again. The voice heard at Mount Sinai, deafening from the start, must be constantly modulated to the human ear. Prophecy—the revelation of revelation, exegesis—is never suppressed or sealed.

The time structure of exegesis, then, is the very temporality of ethics, of the encounter of one with another, "I," and "you." It involves a notion Levinas early in his career called "trace" and later calls "diachrony." Just as the ethical imperative embedded in the disturbing alterity of the other opens up an unanticipated future more future than the projections of the self, so too it bores more deeply into the self than the self's syntheses, however passive; it fissures the self with responsibilities deeper than its recuperative powers of synthesis, its for-itself. The constant deepening or continual elevation of the self effected by ethics is the "theme" of all of Levinas's Talmudic readings—the for-the-other-before-oneself—and this is at work in the very process of exegesis, too. Only in this way, contrary to Derrida's aesthetic misreading of Levinas's thought, can "I" and "you" meet not across violence but pacifically. Language is precisely the pacific medium of an encounter with that which exceeds the terms in encounter with one another. In this way, a text can be a "you." The infinity of exegesis, linked to the pluralism of an ethically constituted humanity and hence to moral tradition, is thus yet another manifestation of the infinity proper to ethics, to the unending and ever greater obligations and responsibilities of persons to and for one another. "The Bible," Levinas writes, "*signifies* for all authentically human thought, for civilization *tout court*, whose authenticity can be recognized in peace, in *shalom*, and in the responsibility of one man for another."[49] A living ethical tradition rests neither on the cold antiquarianism of museum maintenance nor in the fiery but free-floating exuberance of an unbridled avant-garde's permanent revolution or deconstruction. Rather, it means continual renewal through continual inspiration. "We must isolate the ancient examples," Levinas has written, "and extend them to the new situations, principles and categories which they contain."[50]

The all important difference between Levinasian exegesis and Nietzschean interpretation, then, can be stated boldly. Whereas Levinas locates exegesis within an ethico-religious tradition that demands selflessness, the humanist priority of being for the sake of the other before being for oneself, Nietzsche breaks from precisely this tradition—and from all ethico-religious tradition, indeed from all tradition as such—to proclaim the primacy of individual will, and hence the priority of being for the sake of oneself as a willful being over the alleged selflessness of being for the sake of the other (which Nietzsche, quite consistently, interprets as a weak, sick, slavish and sublimated form of selfishness). One can hardly imagine a more radical opposition, recognized by both thinkers. For Nietzsche, as for Derrida, the weight of tradition, as orientation and direction in thinking and life, can only appear as an unwanted and heteronomous violence.

---

[49] "On Jewish Philosophy," Levinas, *In the Time of the Nations*, 172.

[50] "The State of Israel and the Religion of Israel," Levinas, *The Levinas Reader*, 262–63.

Already in 1934, in one of his first philosophical writings, with great precision Levinas links the willful antihumanist spirit of Nietzschean thought—and of Heideggerian thought, which in typical German idealist fashion reifies individual human will into world will (again, the famous "turn," *Kehre*), before whose "voice" humans must humble themselves—to the oncoming horror of Nazism.[51] It is a strong charge, to be sure, but the Holocaust, no less than be-ing, must also be thought deeply, ethically.

Because Levinas renews tradition and Nietzsche rejects it altogether, Nietzschean interpretation radically reverses the value ("revaluation of all values") of all four characteristics of exegesis. While it recognizes the integrity of spirit and matter, it aims at matter to the detriment of spirit. While it recognizes a multiplicity of readings and readers, it aims at their mutual alienation and dispersion, their dissolution, not at the community of *shalom*. While it recognizes the imperative existential force of interpretation, its imperative is from and for-itself alone, not for the greater good that is also the individual good. For Levinasian exegesis, in contrast to Nietzschean interpretation, "the great miracle of the Bible," and by extension all of sacred literature, "lies not at all in the common literary origin, but, inversely, in the confluence of different literatures toward the same essential content . . . the ethical."[52] "We can now appreciate," he writes, "in its full

---

[51] Emmanuel Levinas, "Quelques reflexions sur la philosophie de l'Hitlerisme," in Emmanuel Levinas, *Les imprevus de l'histoire* (Montpellier: Fata Morgana, 1994), 35–41.

[52] Emmanuel Levinas, *Ethics and Infinity*, trans. Richard A. Cohen (Pittsburgh: Duquesne University Press, 1985), 115. Strauss makes a similar point regarding the lack of significance religious consciousness finds "in contradictions and in repetitions which are not intended" in the Bible, but he makes this point not so much in

weight the reference made by the Revelation to exegesis, to the freedom attaching to this exegesis and to the participation of the person listening to the Word, which makes itself heard now, but can also pass down the ages to announce the *same truth* [my italics] in different times."[53] These are not, or need not be, idle or simply beautiful words. But neither are they ontological necessities, allegedly ironclad "laws" of history. Genuine freedom is more difficult, more and less precarious. Texts, like life itself, call for interpretation, and only interpretation awakens texts—not, as Nietzsche thought, to enforce one's own will, to exacerbate one's own isolation, but rather to enter into a living ethico-religious tradition dedicated to all of humankind, dedicated to the unending difficulties of morality and justice, which is nothing less and nothing more than the very process of sanctification, "biblical humanism."[54]

---

the name of the unifying exigency of the ethico-religious tradition than in the name of the epistemological breakdown that necessarily results when a finite mind attempts to understand the doings of the one absolute and hence mysterious God. See Strauss, "On the Interpretation of Genesis," *Jewish Philosophy and the Crisis of Modernity*, 374–75.

[53] Levinas, "Revelation in the Jewish Tradition," *The Levinas Reader*, 195.

[54] Of course Buber also understands the basic Jewish project to be one of "sanctification." Of ethics and sanctification in Levinas, Robert Gibbs has written: "Levinas calls this task ethics, but this is a translation of the Hebrew term *sanctification*," Robert Gibbs, *Correlations in Rosenzweig and Levinas* (Princeton: Princeton University Press, 1992), 187, cited by Alfred I. Tauber (458), in "Outside the Subject: Levinas's Jewish Perspective on Time," in the excellent special Levinas issue subtitled "Levinas's Contribution to Contemporary Philosophy," *Graduate Faculty Philosophy Journal*, vol. 20, no. 2–vol. 21, no. 1: 439–59.

RENEWED THINKING AND SANCTIFIED LIFE

Such a conception of humanism, humanism fully conscious of itself in moral humility, aware of its inexorable link to the divine through exegetical life, would be able finally to reject abstract philosophical notions of freedom—with their dialectical partners: abstract philosophical notions of necessity—upon which certain self-declared "secular humanisms" have built self-distorting ideologies and launched havoc, usurping the name of the highest values. Feuerbach would have been more right than even he knew: genuine humanism would indeed be the expression of humankind's highest aspirations, its highest ideals, but this would in no way sever such idealism from the genuine and demanding transcendence—the transcendence of God—proper to religion. For along with a *humanism* more fully conscious of itself and of its intrinsic religious dimension, would come *religion* also more fully conscious of itself, made aware of its proper and inexorable human dimension. In such a perspective, neither religion nor humanism can do without one another, since neither one nor the other would fully be itself without fully engaging the other—for at bottom they would be inseparable, one. The stakes raised by the question of the meaning and status of humanism are indeed high.

Of course, it is not only the Talmud, such as Levinas reads it in these essays, that raises and suggests these themes. They are central to civilization and hence have been raised in many different contexts in many different ways. There is no problem with philosophy, science, knowledge, per se, except when and insofar as cognition asserts its exclusivity, its hegemony, putting reason before and above revelation, knowledge before and above trust, truth before and above morality, and hence immanence before and impervious to transcendence. Reason is required by ethics, but in the service of ethics. Or, alternatively, if reason is challenged not on ethical but on aesthetic grounds, its abstract exclusivity is merely replaced by another perhaps even more seductive authority, by the shining glory of Homer, by fate and fortune, undermining the difficult freedom of the "image and likeness of God" found in the Bible with the glory, however reverential, of fame and success. Who, after all, speaks for being? One wonders, then, whether Heidegger has really criticized the Bible, whether he has understood its deepest message, when he criticizes self-glorification. Perhaps he has only found a new mask for self-glorification. Or, returning to religious fundamentalists, have they really grasped the provocative transcendence proper to religion, proper to God, when they denounce the humanism launched and sustained by the very Bible they claim to be defending? Levinas's readings will show deeper meanings at work in the reasonableness of reason than the ontological disclosure of what is revealed in truth or the imposition of a being in being. Revelation ethically revealed, continually revealed across the chasm of responsibility separating and joining one from another, "I" from "you," and from "others," opens up the humanity of the human. In so doing, revelation is at work underlying and guaranteeing the veracity of truth.

"Ashes," so Levinas teaches in the third essay that follows, are neither spirit nor matter, but the humility of an Abraham—"I, ashes and dust"—who in the deepest recesses of his self, deeper than his own self, to the point of selflessness, responds to the demands of the other. Abraham remains "our father," the father of humanity, for he has shown a humanity whose dignity, whose "as-for-me," is already "for-the-other," the neighbor.

Richard A. Cohen
October 15, 1998
Charlotte, North Carolina

ONE

The Will of God and the Power of Humanity[1]

According to rabbinic wisdom, nothing is more serious than teaching in the presence of one's masters. The mastery of the teacher and the elevation of the student[2]—and the student's duties—begin whenever even an isolated element of knowledge is communicated from spirit to spirit. Measure

---

[1] LEVINAS: Lesson given before the central Consistory in 1974. [I have translated the title as "The Will of God and the Power of Humanity," though the first part of the title literally reads: "The Will of Heaven" or "The Will of the Sky" (*La Volunté du Ciel*). "Sky" or "Heaven" in this context, based on long Jewish usage, clearly refers to God. Levinas is very much aware, as the following article shows, that this particular verbal indirection or metonomy derives from a Hebrew original. The Hebrew word *"shemayim,"* which also literally means "skies" or "heavens," in religious contexts, such as the one in Levinas's title, refers to God. In the body of the following text, however, I have rendered the French *"ciel"* with the English "heaven," except in two cases when "sky" is clearly meant.]

[2] Levinas's original, *"La maîtrise du maître et l'élévation de l'élève"* plays on the etymological link in French between "mastery" (*"maîtrise"*) and "teacher" (*"maître"*), and between "elevation" (*"élévation"*) and "student" (*"élève"*), both lost in English.

my scruples thus! If I have accepted doing this talmudic reading without the traditional erudition, without the acuity of
spirit that it presupposes or further refines, it is uniquely
with the intention of testifying that an "amateur," provided
he is attentive to ideas, can draw out, even in a superficial
approach to these difficult texts—without which Judaism no
longer is, but texts whose language and interests seem so
strange from the outset that we, Jews today, have some pains
returning to them—some essential suggestions for his intellectual life, on the questions which trouble humanity in every
epoch, that is to say, modern humanity.

But to do this one must take upon oneself to labor upon a
talmudic page, despite all the disadvantages that a somewhat austere public discourse presents.

Without the slightest cost I would certainly be able to lav-
ish assurances regarding the virtues of these texts, by citing
formulations and dicta in which they boast of their own excellence. I want at all costs to avoid this apologetic way of
proceeding. We will have enough to do with the passage whose
translation you have in front of you. Its perspectives mul-
tiply and are enlarged to the measure—or the glorious un-
measure—that one excavates it. The words of the rabbinical
doctors are compared to red hot embers (*Wisdom of the Fathers*, II, 15);[3] they become inflamed when one breathes on
them. Ardor and light are here a matter of breath! The insig-
nificant specks of these embers are illuminated with the

---

[3] Levinas is referring to the third of three sayings by Rabbi
Eliezer ben Horkanos, who is one of five disciples of Rabbi Yohanan
ben Zakkai cited in chapter 2 of *The Wisdom of the Fathers*, a non-
halachic tractate of the Talmud. It reads in full: "Warm yourself by
the fire of the sages, but beware of their glowing coals lest you be
burnt—for their bite is the bite of a fox, their sting is the sting of a
scorpion, their hiss is the hiss of a serpent, and all their words are
like fiery coals."

meaning of which they are the tips. This is also true of the Holy Scriptures. I learned this from Rabbi Chaim of Volozhin, in his *Nefesh Hachaim* [*Soul of Life*].[4] Attribute to my too short breath that which will remain obscure or cold in my remarks. But to retain the comparison, it defines the Book as Book, that is to say, as inspiration.

The translation below is taken from the final pages of the talmudic tractate *Makkot*,[5] a tractate of a little less than fifty pages, hence relatively short. It is devoted to judiciary sanctions—whence whipping or "lashes" (*makkot*)—which follow the transgression of certain interdictions, negative commandments, commandments that say "Thou shalt not," when the transgression had occurred despite the prior warning given to the guilty party and about which witnesses had testified.

A talmudic lesson begins, as you know, with the formulation of several theses, called *Mishnah*.[6] The theses of the

---

[4] Levinas has often praised Rabbi Hayyim Volozhin's work *The Soul of Life*, for which he wrote a preface to the French translation. While this book has not been translated into English in its entirety, the first of its four parts, which is the part to which Levinas most refers, does appear in *An Anthology of Jewish Mysticism*, ed. and trans. Raphael Ben Zion (New York: Yesod Publishers, no date), 133–204, 225–33. See also "'In the Image of God' According to Rabbi Hayyim Volozhiner," in Emmanuel Levinas, *Beyond the Verse: Talmudic Readings and Lectures*, trans. Gary D. Mole (Bloomington: Indiana University Press, 1994), pp. 151– 67, 214–16.

[5] The tractate *Makkot*, literally "lashes," appears in *Nizikin*, literally "Damages," one of the six "Orders" ["*Sidurim*"] into which the Talmud—the Oral Torah—is divided. It continues a discussion of capital and corporeal punishment begun in tractate *Sanhedrin*, named after the ancient central Jewish judicial assembly, which precedes *Makkot* also in *Nizikin*.

[6] Literally "repetition," the Mishnah is the oldest layer of the Talmud, redacted by Rabbi Yehudah HaNasi, circa 200 C.E.

Mishnah, formulated by teachers called *Tanaim*,[7] are enunciated sovereignly and often without reference to Scripture, because they appeal to an oral tradition to which, with the same warrant as the written revelation, a Sinaic origin is attributed. The Mishnah is followed by a text called *Gemarah*,[8] which frequently extends over several pages and which reproduces the discussions and developments raised, among the later rabbinical doctors (from the third to the sixth centuries) called *Amorim*, by the fundamental teachings of the *Tanaim*.

I will be commenting on the final Mishnah of the tractate *Makkot* and a part—about a third—of the Gemarah which follows it (23b). The rest of the Gemarah evokes, in appearance at least, themes other than those which the Mishnah exposes. To be sure, it is often by seeking the overall unity, at first sight disparate, of a so-called talmudic compilation that one discovers the most interesting ideas, and perhaps even the central ideas, guiding it. Today we will have nothing to do with this enthralling but precipitous route. I will just have to refer to one of the two stories which conclude the tractate, whose true meaning is only revealed in terms of their context, which is our text today. Here then is that text, which I have numbered with indented roman numerals in order to be able to refer to it in the commentary.

---

[7] Following the *Zugot*, the "pairs," who taught from about 200 B.C.E. to 20 C.E., the *Tanaim* are the scholars of the generations from about 20 C.E. to 200 C.E., whose contributions make up the Mishnah.

[8] *Gemarah*, literally "completion," is the record of commentary upon the *Mishnah*, discussions which took place both in Babylonia, redacted c. 500 C.E., and known as the *Babylonian Talmud*, and to a lessor extent in Israel, redacted c. 375 C.E. and known as the *Jerusalem Talmud*.

TRACTATE MAKKOT 23a–24b[9]

Mishnah:

I. All those who are liable to excision (by celestial inter-vention), if they have submitted to whipping, are exempt from excision, for it is written (Deuteronomy 25:3): "He shall have inflicted upon him forty lashes, not more; otherwise, in sur-passing this number, one would inflict too many on him and your brother would be debased in your eyes." Once sanctioned, he is as your brother. Such is the opinion of Rabbi Hananiah ben Gamaliel.

II. And Rabbi Hananiah ben Gamaliel says: Since man can lose his life because of a transgression committed, it is by an even greater reason certain that to one who fulfills a com-mandment, life will be granted.

III. Rabbi Shimon says: This can be deduced from the very passage in which one finds the verse (Leviticus 18:19): "For persons acting thus [whoever has committed one of these abominations] will be excised from the bosom of their people." And it is also said (Leviticus 18:5): "You shall thus observe my laws and statutes because the man who practices them obtains life through them. I am the Lord"[10] Therefore, whoever

---

[9] In this and all translations of the Talmud I am following Levinas's French version, which is taken from the "official" trans-lation authorized by the French rabbinical consistory. I have also consulted two English translations, the Soncino translation, *Makkot* in Seder Nezikin: Shebuo'oth and Makkoth, trans. A.E. Silverstone (London: Soncino Press, 1987) and the Brown Judaic Studies trans-lation (*The Talmud of Babylonia: An American Translation*, vol. 24; *Tractate Makkot*, trans. Jacob Neusner (Atlanta: Scholars Press, 1991).

[10] Although the French use the term "Eternal" to translate the four-letter name of God, the tetragrammaton, sometimes translit-erated as "Yahweh"or "Jehovah" (Everett Fox uses "YHWH"), stand-ard usage in English is "Lord," which I have used throughout.

is without transgressing, is rewarded like he who fulfills the commandment.

IV. Rabbi Shimon bar Rabbi[11] says: Does not Scripture state (Deuteronomy 12:23): "But take care to avoid eating blood, for blood is life. . . ." Now, if for blood which naturally repulses man one says that he who abstains from it is rewarded, with even greater reason then for plunder and the transgression of sexual interdictions, which concern that to which human nature aspires and in which it finds pleasure, he who abstains from them would acquire merit, for him and for his posterity, up to the end of all generations.

V. Rabbi Hananiah ben Akashia says: The Holy One, blessed be He, wanted to confer merits on Israel, which is why he gave them the Torah with numerous commandments, because it is said (Isaiah 42:21): "The Lord was pleased, for the triumph of justice, to grant his great and glorious doctrine."

Gemarah:

VI. Rabbi Yohanan has said: The colleagues of Rabbi Hananiah ben Gamaliel do not agree with his way of seeing. Rabbi Ada bar Ahbah says: One teaches at the school: between the Sabbath and the Day of Atonement there is only this difference: voluntary fault for the one is punishable by man, for the other by excision. Now, if it were thus (as Rabbi Hananiah ben Gamaliel wanted), in the two cases the sanction would be in the hands of man.

VII. Rav Nahman bar Isaac replies: This is Rabbi Isaac's teaching. According to him, whipping is not applied to those

---

[11] Rabbi Shimon bar Rabbi is the son of Rabbi Yehuda HaNasi, the redactor of the *Mishnah*, whom the Talmud refers to simply as "Rabbi." (A misprint in the French text erroneously gives his name as "Shimon bar Rami.")

who are liable to excision. For we have a baraitha:[12] *Those who are liable to excision have been named together (in chapter 18 of Leviticus, at the enumeration of the cases of incest which are liable to excision). Why then is incest committed with a sister mentioned separately (Leviticus 20:17)? It is so as to not consider the liability to excision as liability to whipping (which would supposedly have the power of releasing the condemned from excision, excision being the exclusive prerogative of heavenly power).*

VIII. Rabbi Ashi says: You can even say that this teaching is, according to the doctors: the intentional fault of the one [Sabbath] is in the hands of men in principle, the intentional fault of the other [Day of Atonement] depends on Heaven in principle.

IX. Rabbi Adda son of Rabbi Abba says in the name of Rav: In practice one follows the opinion of Rabbi Hananiah be Gamaliel.

X. Rabbi Joseph says: Who then has been above, has returned and said that? Abaye replied to him: Has not Rabbi Joshua ben Levi said: Three things were ruled by the tribunal below, to which the Tribunal above consented. Who has been above, has returned and reported it (telling you)? But these are the verses one interprets. Interpretations thus of verses.

XI. Here is the substance of what Rabbi Joshua ben Levi says: Three things were ruled by the tribunal below to which the heavenly Tribunal consented: a) the reading of the scroll of Esther (at Purim), b) the invocation of the name of God in

---

[12] A *baraitha*, literally "external," is an opinion of a *Tanaim*, who, after the *Zugot*, the "pairs," are the earliest interlocutors of the Talmud, hence an opinion with great weight, but one which was not, however, included as part of the *Mishnah*, the collection edited by Rabbi Yehuda HaNasi.

the greeting given to the neighbor, c) and the bringing of the tithe (owed to the Levites) in the Temple chamber.

XII. For that of the reading of the scroll of Esther, it is written (Esther 9:27): "The Jews, they recognized and accepted." Recognized above what they accepted below.

XIII. For the invocation of the name of God in the greeting, it is written (Ruth 2:4): "Behold Boaz came from Bethlehem, and said to the reapers: 'The Lord be with you.'" And it is written (in Judges 6:12): "The Lord is with you, valiant man." Why this second text? In case one says: Boaz decided this on his own without knowing whether the Heavens consented to his decision, it teaches us this in citing "God is with you, valiant man."

XIV. As to the bringing of the tithe, it is written (Malachi 3:10): "Bring all the tithes into the storehouse, so that there may be food in my house, and put me to the test with that, says the Lord of hosts, [you will see] if I will not open for you the windows of heaven, if I do not put out for you blessing beyond all measure." What does it mean "beyond all measure"? Rabbi bar Raba says: "Until your lips weary of saying 'enough.'"

XV. Eliezer says: Three times the Holy Spirit makes an appearance: at the tribunals of Shem, Samuel of Ramah and King Solomon.

XVI. At the tribunal of Shem, for it is written (Genesis 38:26): "Judah acknowledged them and said: 'She is more just than I.'" How did he know this? Could he not have thought that another than himself had come to her, just as he had come to her? It is because a heavenly voice proclaimed: "Through me are revealed these concealed things."

XVII. At the tribunal of Samuel, for it is written (Samuel 12:3,5): "Very well, accuse me in the face of the Lord and in the face of his anointed, if it is someone's ox or ass I have taken, someone that I have injured or oppressed. . . ." They

answered: "You have not at all injured or oppressed us. . . ."
And he said to them: "God and His elect are witness against
you on this day that you have found nothing to charge against
me." And one answered: "That they are witnesses." Why "one
answers?" Was it not written "they answered?" It is a heav-
enly voice that proclaimed: "I am witness in this affair."

XVIII. At the tribunal of King Solomon, for it is written
(Kings 3:27): "The King thus answered the speech and said:
'Give her the living child and keep from slaying it, she is its
mother.'" How did he know this? Perhaps it was a ruse on his
part? It is that a heavenly voice proclaimed: "She is its mother."

XIX. Raba answered: Is that a proof? Perhaps Judah cal-
culated the months and days and they tallied? One holds by
what is visible. One does not hold by what is invisible. The
same for Samuel, it is all Israel that answered him and this
justified the singular. As when it is written (Isaiah 45:17):
"Israel was saved by the Lord." The same with Solomon, he
deduced it from the one showing love and the other not show-
ing love.

XX. One must rather say it is the tradition that makes
it so.

According to Rabbi Hananiah ben Gamaliel, persons guilty
of transgression which the Pentateuch sanctions by excision
(*kareth*), are freed of this punishment if they receive the whipping imposed on them by the earthly court. "Excision" is in
principle a sanction of death which, according to rabbinic
tradition, is not the business of human courts, but is inflicted
by the heavenly court.

Let us stick for a moment to the language of the Mishnah,
as if there were no need for this language to exceed, by the
thought that bears it, the notions it uses, which at first glance,
to a Parisian of 1974—and intellectually we are all from

Paris—will seem obsolete, particularist, or at least exotic. Their weight of meaning is still considerable, precisely because they remain welded to the examples they generalize and the content they formalize. Thus they have multiple "understandings" which arise not from ambiguity, but from the inexhaustible wealth of the innumerable dimensions of the concrete. Perhaps our Western concepts detach themselves from the concrete prematurely. Oh, the impatience of the concept! Here, the discussion returns ceaselessly to examples, allowing new concepts to germinate from them and setting out again in new directions. But even more—and this is never made explicit enough, which risks perpetuating the impression of a primitive or outdated formalism—this paradigmatic conceptualism is a theoretical procedure for comprehending the Real. It is not translated at each step into behavior and real situations having a documentary significance. Concern for *halakah*, for the concrete rule of conduct, is certainly essential there. It derives from paradigmatic conceptualism, but requires an additional decision. At the theoretical level where the Gemarah takes place, however, the dialectic is free. These notions welded to the concrete leave to the play of theory a field different than that wherein the concepts of a pure abstraction move. They are not at all reduced to anecdotes, no more than are certain notions of modern physics reducible to the images and schemas by which one conveys them in our high school textbooks.

Human courts thus would deal with the faults which cast us out of the human and would repair the irreparable. Can a court do as much as mercy or Grace can do? Is Grace manifest at court? Forget for an instant the disgraceful image of whipping, forget the violence of excision and the formalism of the judicial procedure. The notion of lashes indicates a human sanction whose essence would consist precisely in touching the intangible personal dignity of the neighbor.

Where does Grace fit into this! But the reference to Deuteronomy 25:3 is explicit: it is here that love of the neighbor must give all it can give, sanction without degrading, interfere in the affairs of the other without touching his freedom. Are not the court and justice this extreme measure of a difference which is a differential?

Defined here by concepts as unpleasant as whipping, human justice substitutes itself for the rigorous verdict of the Absolute: "He will be excised from his people." Excision from life, but also from Israel, which is to say from the human order, from the order of true humanity, from true society. And, according to Maimonides, who in the twelfth century extracted the substance of the Talmud, excision from the future world, from the ultimate finality of the human and from the World in relation to which messianic promises mark only a penultimate stage. Rabbi Hananiah breaks with the gloomy mythological fatality whose eventuality would indicate a religious tyranny, in order to proclaim that with regard to Heaven fault does not exist which—between men and in clarity—one could not expiate or make expiatable. The court, an assembly freed of the blind pulsions of existence, elevated to disinterestedness, would be the place where the regenerative divine will manifests itself—in the form of the fraternal, a paternal initiative.

Rabbi Hananiah ben Gamaliel's argument itself is quite remarkable. It seems to play on words. In reality, Deuteronomy's reference to the expression "your brother" is not a game. It is a reason and definition of justice. An act without the spirit of vengeance, contempt, or hate—an act without passion, to be sure. But positively, a fraternal act. It arises from a responsibility for the other. To be responsible for the neighbor, to be the other's keeper—contrary to the Cainian vision of the world—defines fraternity. It is at the court, which reasons and weighs, that love of the neighbor would be possible.

Excess whose sense is visible: no indulgence is gratuitous. It is always paid by an innocent person without his knowledge. One is only allowed to judge if one personally assumes the price.[13] But it depends on the earthly judge, on man, on the brother of the guilty, to restore the neighbor to human fraternity. Being responsible for his brother right up to being responsible for his freedom! Which can only occur by means of violence in the pain that awakens, that is to say, instructs and educates and tests. Maimonides will insist on the necessity of repentance, there as well, but pardon—the return to the human—is only possible after sanction. Heteronomy would therefore be among the conditions of autonomy, and would be thought by Judaism with acuity under the concept—or under the category—of paternity.[14]

Divine justice itself would have to be manifest in an earthly court to cloth itself in human fraternity. One has five hundred times more confidence in this mercy or grace than in pure strictness. And as a matter of fact the second argument of Rabbi Hananiah ben Gamaliel (*II*), an a fortiori argument, is implicitly based on this confidence. Is it not written (Exodus

---

[13] LEVINAS: "The judge has pronounced his judgment; he has acquitted the innocent and condemned the guilty, and he saw that it is a poor man who must pay, so he reimbursed the latter with his personal money. This is justice and charity . . ." Tractate *Sanhedrin* 6b [French translation by Grand-Rabbi Salzer, p. 27].

[14] LEVINAS: It is against the paganism of the "Oedipal complex" notion that one must think forcefully the apparently purely edifying verses such as Deuteronomy 8:5: "You shall thus consider in your conscience that the Lord, your God, chastises you like a father chastises his son." Paternity has here the signification of a constitutive category of meaning and not its alienation. On this point, at least, psychoanalysis attests the profound crisis of monotheism in contemporary sensibility, a crisis which does not come down to the refusal of some dogmatic propositions. It harbors the ultimate secret of anti-semitism.

34:7): "The Lord . . . preserves his favor for thousands of generations; He bears crime, rebellion, sin, but He absolves them not at all. He pursues the iniquity of the fathers on their children and grandchildren, to the third and fourth descendants. . . ." And the rabbis gloss this: for thousands of generations—two thousand, at least. For two thousand generations, at least, the favor accorded to merit is transmitted; for four generations iniquity cries for justice. Divine mercy is thus at least five hundred times stronger than its strictness. Beyond this theological arithmetic lies a moral optimism: from the victory won over evil nothing is ever lost, while the victory of evil must come to an end.[15] Hence Rabbi Hananiah will say: If the transgression of an interdiction was able to "excise" a human person from his people, so much the more the fulfillment of a commandment must give back the life of he who is liable to *kareth* and restore him to his people. So, to submit to the whipping decided on by the court is, objectively, a fulfillment of the law to which the guilty party is subject.

Submitting in repentence, the violence of the court equivocates into the fulfillment of a commandment—is this not the implicit premise of Rabbi Hananiah ben Gamaliel's a fortiori argument, which calls forth the contribution of Rabbi Shimon (*III*)? Certain interpreters see in it a teaching independent of what Rabbi Hananiah ben Gamaliel sets forth on the importance of interdictions. Our reading, which endeavors to link itself to the beginning of the Mishnah, justifies at least

---

[15] LEVINAS: True civilization is a force, but it must begin. Did it not begin naturally? This is the entire question posed by the crisis of our civilization. Is not perversion included in the natural, the spontaneous, the naive? Must there not be a (paternal) violence to get an act of freedom and disinterestedness? And what about impenitent evil?

an affinity between these two texts. Constraint imposed on the spontaneity of life—such as it manifests itself in the negative commandments of Leviticus, the sexual interdictions appearing as prototypes or at least as privileged exemplars of the negative commandments—is affirmed by Rabbi Shimon as a guarantee of life: "Whoever is there without transgressing is rewarded as he who fulfills the commandments."

So the negative commandment—whatever the positive steps implicated in its fulfilment—is constraint par excellence, pure constraint. It is so through its imperative form and its content, since it commands a constraint be imposed on life lived in its living vitality, exacted from life lived as "a force on the go." Negative commandments, restraining life and, notably, restraining the blind profusion of sexual desire, nonetheless would be promoters of life, so believes Rabbi Shimon.

And one can indeed see good faith in that promise which the faith of the simple person awaits: longevity or eternal life, reward for the abstinence ordered by interdictions. But one can also understand by life precisely this limitation of life's savage vitality—something which circumcision would symbolize, a limitation through which life awakens from its somnambulant spontaneity, sobers up from its nature, and interrupts its centripetal movement, to open itself to otherness and the other. Life in which one can recognize the destiny of the Jewish people who, limiting that wild vitality by the law, accepts this limitation as its best part, that is to say, as a "reward."

And one can understand by the life menaced with *kareth*, with excision outside one's people, and by the life restored to one who has submitted to the constraint decided by the court, a life contrary to that of a being inebriated by its own nature, when, to the unlimited encroachment by the appetite for desire, for domination, and for enjoyment, to which nothing is an obstacle, not even the other, a plenitude of meaning, a responsibility for justice, is substituted.

Even now, in the unbridled life that the negative commandment must reduce to the human, one hears the triumphant din of Rome (whose echo traverses the last part of the tractate (24a–24b) that we will not be commenting on today), the din which, in times of fatigue, times when one is on the road, makes one doubt the justice of the just life of masters like Rabbi Gamaliel, Rabbi Eliazer and Rabbi Joshua, the justice of the just life in which Rabbi Akiva alone is still able to laugh.[16]

Rabbi Shimon bar Rabbi deduces the "reward" reserved for those who do not transgress negative commandments from the promises regarding the consumption of blood. If the abstinence conforming to a natural repulsion is rewarded, so much the more the resistance opposed to the desirable! The horror of blood has here perhaps a signification which derives not only from the gastronomical order. Resistance to sexual dissipations and to a taste for looting is meritorious a fortiori. Still, this is the true life, to believe in the civilization of the great metropolises and also the great literatures! All that bookkeeping of merits and rewards has a larger signification. The vital life, the natural life, perhaps begins in a

---

[16] LEVINAS: "One day Rabbi Gamaliel, Rabbi Eliazer, Rabbi Joshua and Rabbi Akiva found themselves on the road. They heard the din of the city of Rome, the Capital, at a distance of one hundred and twenty miles. They looked at one another and cried, but Rabbi Akiva laughed. They asked: Why do you laugh? He asked them: Why do you cry? They said: Those villains who worship false gods and burn incense to idols live in peace and taste tranquility, but the House, the altar steps of our Lord is burned. How come we do not cry? He said to them: It is for this that I laugh. Those who would thwart his will are like that [peaceful and tranquil]. All the more reason us." [*Makkot* 24a–24b. This is the first of the two stories at the end of *Makkot* that Levinas does not comment upon.]

naivete and in repugnancies agreeing with ethics; it ends in compliance with loveless debauchery and looting erected into a social condition, into exploitation. Human life begins where this vitality, innocent in appearance, but virtually destructive, is mastered by interdictions. Does not authentic civilization, whatever be the biological echoes or the political defects it brings to pass, consist in holding back the breath of naive life and thus awakening "for posterity and to the end of all generations"?

Now we understand the thought of Rabbi Hananiah ben Akashia (V) with which the Mishnah concludes.

The Lord wanted to confer merits on Israel by multiplying his commandments. Not of course to produce artificial merits, nor to put obstacles on its path. It is the greatness of justice and its glory that interdictions are necessary against that life which is lived as a force on the go. Even there where, as in the horror one can experience in consuming or even in shedding blood, nature seems to protect us from evil. However, there is no natural inclination healthy enough to be unable to get involved. Holiness is necessary for the well being of the healthy.[17] Hence one must have it even when at the outset instinct protects us from harming others, when it is innocent.

But the greatness of justice, which is the issue in this final part of the Mishnah, and which conditions a life obedient to multiple commandments, is also the glory of the court and judges. Rendering the doctrine glorious: only judges who themselves practice the multiple commandments can form the glorious assembly where the will of God is implemented. The judge is not merely a jurist expert in the laws; he obeys those laws which he applies, and the study of the laws is also

---

[17] *"La sainteté est nécessaire à la santé du sain."*

the essential form of this obedience. Such a situation is necessary for the violence of whipping to reduce "excision," for the responsibilities of one for the other and structures— ontologically strange—to be able to assume, in inflicting a sanction, the being of the other. Only thus can there be a value anterior to freedom that does not destroy freedom, which is probably the primary signification of the exceptional word: God.

HEAVEN AND EARTH

The earthly court intervening in sanctions which concern only Heaven—is this the secularization of the Torah, the annulment of what the philosophers call divine transcendence?

So the text of the Gemarah begins by recalling opinions which seem to oppose the decision of Rabbi Hananiah ben Gamaliel (*VI, VII, VIII*), even though this report ends with the testimony of Rabbi Ada son of Rabbi Ahbah. In judicial practice one follows the opinion of Rabbi Hananiah ben Gamaliel (*IX*). There exists, one says, a teaching of the school according to which the difference between Yom Kippur and Shabbat derives from the fact that the transgression of the interdictions of the one is of concern only to Heaven, and the transgression of the interdictions of the other is answerable to the court of men (*VI*). That the metaphysical problem of the difference between transcendence and immanence is not detached from questions posed by the interdictions sanctioning the transgression of interdictions is quite remarkable and characteristic of a thought whose concepts receive their ultimate sense from an ethical context.

But how is this "teaching of the school" accommodated to the decision of Rabbi Hananiah? Rav Nahman bar Isaac (*VII*) recognizes in this "teaching of the school" the extremist thesis of Rabbi Isaac. The latter insists on the difference between the divine and the human derived from the irreducibility of "excision" to whipping. As a matter of fact, one text specifically links excision to incestuous relations between brothers and sisters (Leviticus 20:17),[18] even though this sanction had already been exacted for incestuous relations in general (Leviticus 18:29).[19] The repetition would prove the irreducibility of excision! Rabbi Isaac is opposed to granting a regenerative whipping to he who has been excised. It is obviously quite important that Rabbi Isaac's opinion be invoked here: it is the denial of a purely humanist and naturalist interpretation of the Law. We will return to it shortly.

Regarding the "teaching of the school" just evoked, the "doctors" would have given another lesson (*VIII*): in principle the intentional sin liable to excision falls within the scope of Heaven. But, in fact, on this excision, which in principle concerns only Heaven, the human court would be able to act. Is this slackness, given "human weakness?" Or is there not a rigorous thought behind this intellectual "making do?" Does not the transcendence and, in the etymological sense, the excellence of the heavenly Court include in its very emphasis an elevation which would be a descent toward man? It is in this sense that we have read the Mishnah. Absolute justice would of itself become mercy, not in an unchecked and unjustified indulgence, but across the human court. God . . . would be a mercy born in justice and in the rigor of justice, which would signify concretely: the mediation of an assembly

---

[18] Leviticus 20:17: "A man who shall take his sister, the daughter of his father or the daughter of his mother, and he shall see her nakedness and she shall see his nakedness, it is a disgrace and they shall be excised in the sight of the members of their people; he will have uncovered the nakedness of his sister, he shall bear his iniquity."

[19] Leviticus 18:29: "For whoever commits any of these abominations, the people who do so will be excised from among their people."

of just men, the very possibility of such an assembly. And, inversely, is not the assembly of the just itself at the natural source of His judgment; in it another will is intended, its judgment is inspired and exceeds the purely human human condition. This is what our text will say further on (*XV* to *XX*). Justice is not decided in order to establish or restore itself. The immanent system of laws is weighed down and always overwhelmed by an exigency coming from elsewhere.

But his would be considered a violence of the supernatural, an alienation, by those who see in the self-sufficiency of the identical the ultimate figure of the free and rational. Unless—irreducible as the principle of excision is in keeping the guilty within the power of the Court on high—what is expressed here is a unique heteronomy that is not corrupted; unless this violence does not deserve the name of violence one so eagerly gives to it, for it precedes the freedom animating only the pneumatism of the soul; unless prophecy is the essence of the human, the traumatism that awakens it to freedom; unless, in the permanence of this traumatism, lived as fear of God—neither terror nor fear of everyday commonness—is freed the freedom of a vigilance wrestling with the slumber of the ego preoccupied with itself. It is in such a traumatism that one can understand, not metaphysically but properly so-called, the word "transcendence," disrupting the world which, as a world, is the reign of the identical and which suffices unto itself within the system. Man as the Same upset or animated by the Other is an irreducible structure or category of the Other-in-the-Same. Against the Greco-Roman model of the Same posited as primitive or ultimate, as a term self-sufficient unto itself, the human court assumes full responsibility only because it is a responsibility animated by the other than itself. The will of God is all high to the extent that it is fulfilled in the human court. Its prophetic manifestation where it descends toward man, and is expressed by him, is probably not just any movement, but its supreme elevation. Numerous biblical and talmudic texts have made this familiar to us.[20]

That the opinions mentioning the irreducibility of excision have not been omitted in our text thus indicates that justice is not a system whose rationality commands men and gods without differentiating them, a system that would be revealed in human legislation as the structures of space are shown in the theorems of geometricians, the justice that a Montesquieu calls the "logos of Jupiter," seeming by this metaphor to recuperate religion, even though, effacing the difference, he secularizes transcendence. In the justice of the rabbis, the difference conserves its proper sense. The ethical is not the corollary of the religious. It is, of itself, the element in which religious transcendence can have a meaning.[21]

TRANSCENDENCE AND INSPIRATION

If the decision of Rabbi Hananiah ben Gamaliel does not annul the beyond, how can we be assured that Heaven agrees

---

[20] LEVINAS: For example, in a striking way, Psalm 113, with which *Hallel* [Praises] opens. The divine elevation "grows" in the first five verses and then suddenly—hyperbole of this elevation—the glory of the Lord becomes a look which peers down deeper and deeper, and an act which goes from the poverty (verse 7) to the despair (verse 9) of humans. [Translator's note. Psalm 113, verse 7: "He raises up the poor out of the dust, and lifts the needy out of the ashheap"; verse 9: "He makes the barren woman to keep house, and be a joyful mother of children. Haleluya!"]

[21] LEVINAS: That the traumatism undergone by the Same, under the blow of the divine Other through which some justice is established between men responsible and accountable to one another, is also the best part of Israel's destiny and, by way of alertness, the embrace of God. It is also the meaning of the two stories with which the tractate *Makoth* ends.

with this decision? A simplistic question whose scope is considerable.

The way in which this assurance will be discovered here (*X* to *XIV*) permits us to elucidate a meaning of the beyond which breaks with the mythological infantilism of a quasi-spatial separation, of the other-world of heavens inhabited by beings "on a grand scale," of a relation with the beyond understood as an exchange of information, with a god who would merely be one power among powers, capable of assuring the success or failure of men. All this is certainly suggested by the question of Rabbi Joseph: "Who has gone above, has returned and reported?" Can the Mosaic revelation itself, as an historical fact, bear up against this? Who attests after all to its authenticity? Rabbi Joseph's question goes that far.

It is then that Abaye, taking up again a saying of Rabbi Joshua ben Levi (*X*), confers on the interpretation of Scriptural verses, on hermeneutics, on *Midrash*, the power to force the secret of transcendence.

Three things, according to Joshua ben Levi, enacted by the court below, were in agreement with the heavenly Court (XI): the institution of the reading of the scroll of Esther on Purim, even though Moses obviously was not able to institute it; the right to evoke the Name of God in greeting one's neighbor, even though this name must not be pronounced in vain; the depositing in the Temple of the tithe dedicated to the Levites and priests, even though the Law of Moses did not foresee the mediation of the Temple.

One would know that these human institutions had received the agreement of Heaven through the interpretation of the verses which inform us of these institutions and which confirm them.

For the reading of Esther (*XII*), it is written: "The Jews instituted and accepted" (Esther 9:27). Why these two words, except to signify: one certified above what they accepted below. The right to invoke the name of God in greeting the neighbor (*XIII*)? The decision of Boaz (a judge, for the book of Ruth begins with "It was at the time of the judges . . .") in Ruth (2:4), confirmed (anachronistically) by "the Lord is with you, valiant man" with which an angel greeted Gideon (Judges 6:12); bringing the tithe to the Temple (*XIV*), instituted by Nehemiah (10:40), is confirmed by Malachi (Malachi 3:10).

How can such answers—planted in the bosom of a downright *petitio principii*—measure up against the radicalism of Rabbi Joseph's question? It is certainly permitted to understand them as the expression of a position. The biblical canon invested with an exceptional authority, without requiring new revelations, would contain, for he who knows how to interpret its verses, an answer to everything.

But in the final account does not Rabbi Joseph's question also concern the man of whom it has been said: "Go up on the mountain and tarry there, I will give you tablets of stone, the doctrine and the precepts, etc." (Exodus 14:12)? Does not Abaye's answer adduce for us a more current lesson? Does not the interpretation of Scripture have a spiritual bearing by itself? The verses commented upon, instead of resting on the authority of Scripture, are they not meant to establish it?

In fact, the adventure of the Midrash, the very possibility of hermeneutics, in its rigorously formal advance, do they not already belong to the very way in which another voice is heard among us—the very way of transcendence, as one says in terms of the school. Let's forget the historical circumstances about which the verse bears the trace and the data one could draw out of it. Let's restore the sense of what is said by the texture of the text. The rabbinical doctors liked to stick to the letter. It is perhaps necessary thus to invoke all the dead weight of the signs which weigh down and dull signification. But expression does not come back to the simple transmission of thoughts. The expression of signification belongs to its very significance, to the strange fecundity of the intelligible, through which there is spirit, that is, inspiration. As if the sense of a thought were carried—meta-phor—beyond the end which limits the intention of the thinker. It is said farther than his Said. It is said outside of the sayer. Its folded wings or the germ of innumerable lives promised in it—seminal reasons—are also lodged in the letters of the text—metaphors of a thought exceeding what it thinks. This whole literature— in the sense in which one says "fillister" or "masts"[22]—awaits or inspires the reading. The verses cry out: "Interpret me." Such is the inspiration of all authentic literature, defining the book as book—it guides the history of nations.

But inspiration is not only in language when it rises to the Book and surpasses its instrumental function of transmitting data—inasmuch as language can do this—and when, inspired, it inspires. Interchange from one person to the other, irreducible to the transmission of data, assuring the coherence of an order of things, is produced, to be sure, in the interpretation of a meaning. But all literature does not go back to the primary ground of meaning, is not the foundation of meaning. Where does this foundation occur? Would

---

[22] The significance of "fillister" [*feuillure*] and "masts" [*mature*] is unclear in this context. Both terms are singular plurals, like "fish" or "moose," in English, and are somewhat archaic in French usage, like "thou" and "hast" in some English Bible translations. Perhaps Levinas is suggesting that such stylistic turns are sufficient to solicit commentary. Alternatively, perhaps, Levinas is making a reference—lost to nonparticipants—to a prior paper or discussion from the 1974 Colloquium of French-speaking Jewish Intellectuals, where his own paper was presented as the keynote and final address.

this not be the privilege of the Scriptures to which Abaye referred? Is there a sense or story, a said, a fable, that does not tell of the relation of man to man? Is there a relation of man to man which does not take the ego out of itself, which does not break the identity of the identical through which the living clutch their being? Is there a relation of man to man which is not ethical? The ethical is not a region or an ornament of the real, it is of itself disinterestedness itself, which is only possible under the traumatism in which presence, in its impenitent equanimity of presence, is upset by the Other. Upset or awakened. To prove the authenticity and value of this traumatism is again to return to this very traumatism, to that transcendence or wakefulness where all these "notions" signify for the first time for us.

In the texts invoked, in fact, specific situations and beings—equal to themselves, held within definitions and frontiers which integrate them into an order and make them rest in a world—are traversed by a breathe which rouses and agitates their sluggishness, or their identity of beings and things, wrenching them from their order without alienating them. This is the miracle of beings lounging in their being and awakening to new deeper and more sober awakenings. One cannot doubt it: this is the miracle, as disturbance of order, as rending of the Same by the Other, which remains the structure—or the de-structure—of transcendence. And if the miracles of pure thaumaturgy seem to us spiritually suspect and admissible as simple figures of the divine epiphany, it is not because they alter the order, but because they do not alter it enough, because they are not miracles enough, because in them the Other awakening the Same is not other enough.

Curiously, the first biblical passage cited (XII) by Rabbi Joshua ben Levi in favor of agreement between the human court and the heavenly Court, and which thus would maintain the difference between Heaven and Earth, as well as an

agreement between them—that is to say, prophetic monotheism—, is the text of Esther, from which God, one could
say, has withdrawn right up to his name, right up to the
word through which one designates him. But it is here that
His inspiration bursts into the middle of the events which
the book of Esther relates in their immanent motivation and
in the necessities and chances (*purim*) of fate.[23] That, in the
liturgical instauration of Mordechai and Esther, these events
could have been understood as events of Holy history is the
miraculous surplus of their belonging to the divine plan. The
historical order—the established order—awakens to the ethical order at the culminating moment of the drama, when
Esther upsets the royal situation, wholly regulated and regular, and, to save other men, consents to her own ruin. Disrup-
tion of order or awakening which balances and corresponds
to the king's insomnia.[24] A midrashic text of the tractate
Megillah compares the insomnia of Ahashuarus to the very
insomnia of God, as if across this impossibility of sleeping a
vigil or absolute sobriety bursts into being.

No less remarkable is the second text (*XIII*), where the
epiphany of God is invoked in the appearance of a human

---

[23] The apparently Persian word *"purim,"* after which the Jewish
holiday of *Purim* is named, according to the text of the Scroll of
Esther seems to mean "lots." Within the Esther narrative it refers
to the lots thrown by King Ahasuerus's (usually identified with King
Xerxes, 486–465 B.C.E.; though identified by the Septuagint with
King Artaxerxes, his successor) viceroy Haman, enemy of the Jews,
to select an auspicious day upon which to destroy all the Jews of
the Persian empire. The name of God does not appear in the Story
of Esther, which is read as part of the liturgy on the Jewish holiday
of Purim.

[24] Unable to sleep, the king reads in the royal chronicles that
Mordechai had earlier saved his life. Thus begins Mordechai's rise
and Haman's decline in the king's favor.

face. In the face, the irreducible difference of the beyond bursts between what is given to me and is understood and belongs to my world, and what, under the order thus constituted, absents itself, disquiets and awakens.

The third moment (*XIV*), the transformation of the donation of the tithe, is it not a transformation of giving itself into a generosity, trusting in an institution, but where the donor does not know his beneficiary or his gratitude? And is this not one of the significations of the cult? What "strong spirits" would be tempted to make fun of as an obligation to an empty Sky [*Ciel vide*] is, enigmatically, the absolute openness of the soul. Openness of dis-inter-estedness, of sacrifice without recompense, of discourse without echo, which "trust in God" and prayer imply. Openness toward the infinite which cannot be confirmed by any response, if not by its own psychological disproportion. It is an abundance to which lip service cannot suffice, according to the rabbinical hermeneutics, so strange, at the end of Malachi 3:10.[25] Beyond discourse, there is an abundance of reward in the abundance of giving.

---

[25] Malachi 3:10: "Bring all the tithes into the storehouse, so that there may be food in my house, and put me to the test with that, says the Lord of hosts, if I will not open for you the windows of heaven, and put out for you blessing immeasurable." This text is part of the *haftorah* (reading from the prophets) read each year on the "Great Sabbath" [*Shabbat Hagadol*], the Sabbath before Passover. Regarding the "strange" rabbinical hermeneutics, I have been informed by the French mathematician and talmudist Professor Georges Hansel (who also happens to be Levinas's son-in-law) as follows: going beyond the straightfoward but simple idea of a reward of great economic abundance, in several places the Talmud (Shabbat 32b; Taanit 9a & 22b; Makkot 23b) interprets the last three words of this verse (Hebrew: *ad bli dai*) translated above as "immeasurable," to mean that one will be so overwhelmingly satisfied that one's lips will wither saying "enough" (Hebrew: *dai*).

INSPIRATION AS SPIRIT

Were we right to elucidate inspiration—the Other in the Same, the Other instructing or awakening the Same—as the spirituality of the spirit? Were we right to recognize in the ethical, at the level of the court which is an assembly of the just, the very place where spirit breathes? For this to be so, would it not have been necessary to have interpreted as inspiration the very reasons of the reasoning Reason in which philosophy, in its logic, recognizes the reign of the Identity that nothing other could either trouble or guide?

Now this is precisely what the final part of our text intends to suggest to us. Here are three passages known to every reader of the Bible: in the first (*XVI*), Judah, son of Jacob, recognizes the injustice of his accusation against Tamar (court of Shem). In the second (*XVII*), the people of Israel recognize the disinterestedness of the prophet Samuel, its judge (court of Samuel). In the third (*XVIII*), king Solomon recognizes who is the mother between two women who are disputing over a child (court of Solomon). Three situations in which the Gemarah introduces the voice of Heaven. To be sure, this voice penetrates into the court, drawn from the voices which at the first—and at the last—reading of the text are human: Judah's, who recognizes his error; the people's, who testify; the king's, who judges. And this is already remarkable: the voice of God is a human voice, inspiration and prophecy in the speech of men.

To be sure, the Gemarah is bent on finding in the propositions upon which the word of God is "charged" an ambiguity and "uncertainties," despite the firmness of resolve visibly attributed by the Bible—read naively—to the human personages. But it is the Gemarah that opposes a scepticism to its own reasons (*XX* and *XXI*): the avowal of he who recognizes his injustice, the unanimous testimony of a people, the wisdom of the judge, are they not explicable by pure reason? Yet nonetheless the final word consists in referring to a tradition (*XX*) attesting to the "heavenly voice." Does not the Gemarah thus suspect an insurmountable ambiguity in the exercise of pure reason? Every logos would require inspiration! There would be difference and traumatism, teaching and wakefulness in every evidence! A paternal "Other," which does not alienate, in every identity! Thus we link up with the initial theme of transcendence at the bosom of the court's decision, penetration of the divine within the world across human propheticism, or conservation of the divine measure of excision, and the difference between divine will and human will, in the very humanization of divine strictness.

MODERN RELIGIOUS PROPRIETY

In concluding, may I ask you to admire once again the marvelous audacity of the sentence which serves as the very hinge of our text (*X*): "Who has gone over there, returned and reported it?"

The end of a certain theology and of a certain religion. The whole liberation, but also the whole gloomy ennui—a matter to be overcome—of modern humanity. Lucidity which renders quite intolerable the discourse in which one speaks in an infantile way as if someone had really returned from over there to tell us what happens there, as if the myth of Er of Pamphylia which Plato relates in Book X of *The Republic* were a travel story. But, above all, as if transcendence were only an exchange of data with an other-world where once again an experience occurs in the beyond, coming to augment the baggage of our knowledge and to keep us as an identical being, the same, consolidated in its identity through its experiences, synthesized and synchronized as experiences.

And what profound ambiguity in the response which refers us to the commentary of Scripture! Is not the response as ironic as it is pious? Would the relation of transcendence push its path through human effort? For the extraordinary Sinaic revelation, for the voice of God resounding in thunder but which would no longer be persuasive, one substitutes a pedantic commentary, possibly duped by all the impostures of the century, a flood of paper! Are the impenetrable heavens going to be ripped open on the benches of the *yeshiva* where one comments on commentaries of commentaries referring precisely to the revealed text to which Rabbi Joseph's question applies, and about which other sages will have for a long time suggested its contingency in terms of the vicissitudes and experiences of the story of which it would be the document?

Ironic moment which one must not take lightly. It thwarts our idea of modern man, it stops it, if only for an instant. This irony is certainly justified, if the exegesis of Scripture is strictly bound to seeking the entry into some Heaven on the momentum of traditional proofs for the existence of God. It is an irony which also overtakes so-called critical readers who fancy they are dealing with the Book's meaning when they denounce in it blind alleys to the beyond; for these critical readers equally, transcendence continues to signify an exchange of data with God or an experience of the supernatural. Having descended to the underground of verbal signs, criticism has lost, under an artificial but apparently sufficient illumination, the philosophical certainties, right up to the desire to leave the Cave.

In the face of the abundance of printed documents that we use, we have perhaps forgotten what reading is. We are no longer acquainted with the difference that distinguishes the Book from documentation. In the former there is an inspiration purified of all the vicissitudes and all the "experiences" that had been its occasion, offering itself as Scripture whereby each soul is called to exegesis, which is both regulated by the rigorous reading of the text and by the unicity—unique in all eternity—of it's own contribution, which is also its discovery, the soul's share. It is in this sense that a great master has taught us to read the liturgical formula: "Give us our share in your Torah."[26]

Irony which is not a euphemism for negation. It expresses the modesty of a spiritual alternation and even an alternation of alternations before the letters of Scripture. Sometimes these letters maintain—for those who believe in them as well as for those who scoff at them—the dogmatism of a superior power intervening in Nature; and sometimes they strike both believers and scoffers, awakening them from their customs. And in this awakening there is an alternation of movements: from traumatism to the literature and grammar which already reestablish order, and then a movement from philology to the understanding of a meaning which once again affects and disturbs, wrenching from the bed of the natural preformations which protect and reassure. Ambiguity in which not only our lack of faith wavers, but the diachrony of a soul which finds itself cramped in the synchrony of the syntheses whereby the transcendence of inspiration cannot be proven without inflicting by the same token a contradiction.

Also destroyed in it is the humanism of a Renaissance man, the superior natural being, welcoming and contesting supernatural experience. In this ambiguity a humanity appears

---

[26] This statement—"Grant us our share in Your Torah."—appears in the traditional Jewish liturgy directly after the conclusion of the most central prayer of Judaism, called the "Eighteen Benedictions" or the "Standing" prayer or, even more simply (in the Talmud), the "Prayer," which is said at least three times daily.

whose spirit is inspiration and prophecy. Prophecy which is not some happy accident of the spirit, a "genius," but its very spirituality:[27] an affection of self and others stronger than the receptivity which waits for it, a listening, an understanding surpassing the capacity of hearing, impossible possibility—or miracle—the most hidden, of human existing and perhaps the very manner in which the spirit penetrates nature.

---

[27] LEVINAS: It is in this sense certainly that the prophet Amos (3:8) attributes his prophetic gift to his very hearing: "The Lord God has spoken, who would not prophecize?" But watch out for the false prophets! More prudently than Amos, the greatest of the prophets [Moses], in Numbers (11:27), learning that "Eldad and Medad prophecize in the camp," wishes that all men accomplishing their anthropological essence ("all the people of God") could prophecize. This is a vow and a prayer like the liturgical formula cited above ["Give us our part in your Torah"]. Men must have teachers, schools, philology and History. But the danger of false prophets is certainly not reason enough to remain troglodyte.

Two

Beyond the State in the State[1]

Tractate Tamid 31b–32b[2]

Alexander of Macedon posed ten questions to the elders of the Negev [the south].

[1] He asked them if the distance is greater from heaven to earth than from east to west. They answered: From east to west it is greater. You know that when the sun is in the east, everyone to the west can look at it, and when it is in the west, everyone to the east can also look at it. Whereas when the sun

---

[1] LEVINAS: This lesson was originally given at the 29th Colloquium of [French Speaking] Jewish Intellectuals, December 5, 1988.

[2] LEVINAS: This text follows, with some breaks, the excellent translation by Arlette Elkaim-Sartre, extracts of *Aggadoth du Talmud de Babylone* (Lagrasse: Editions Verdier, 1982), pp. 1344–1347. [Translator's note: I have also consulted the Brown Judaic Studies translation, *The Talmud of Bablylonia: An American Translation, Vol. XXXV, Meilah and Tamid*, trans. by Peter J. Haas (Atlanta: Scholars Press, 1991).]

is in the middle of the sky, no one can look at it. The sages nevertheless think that the two distances are equal, for it is said: "For as the heavens are high above the earth, so His goodness is great for those who fear Him; as distanced as the Orient is from the Occident, so He distances from us our transgressions" (Psalms 103:11). Why can no one look at the sun when it is in the middle of the firmament? Because absolutely nothing obstructs the view.

[2] What has been created first, the heavens or the earth? Answer: the heavens, for it is said: "In the beginning, God created the heavens and the earth" (Genesis 1:1).

[3] He asked them: What has been created first, light or darkness? One answered him: This question has not yet been decided. Why did they not answer him that it is the darkness that came first? The elders thought that Alexander was about to ask them questions about what is below, what is behind and what is before.—But in that case they should not have answered the question about the heavens! At the start, they believed that he just happened upon that question and that he would not pose others of the same type. When he posed the question about light and dark, they decided to no longer answer, for fear that he would come to ask them, indeed, what is above and what is below, what is interior, what is exterior.

[4] He asked them: What is the definition of the sage? They answered him: The sage is he who foresees what will happen.

[5] He said to them: Who do you call strong? They said: He who masters his evil inclination.

[6] He said to them: Who do you call rich? They answered: He who is content with the share which is allotted to him.

[7] He asked them: What should one do to live? Kill oneself.—And what should one do to die?—Let live.

[8] He asked them: What should one do to be popular?— Hate power and authority.—I have a better answer than yours.

One must love power and authority and take advantage of them to do favors for the people.

[9] Is it better to live on land or on sea?—On land, because all those who risk going to sea only regain their tranquility when they have landed on firm land.

[10] Who among you is wisest? We are all equal, since we have all answered your questions as one man.

[11] Why do you oppose us? They answered simply: Satan is a conqueror. He is always a conqueror.—I can have you executed by a royal decree!—Power is in the hands of the king, but it does not befit a king to lie. Forthwith he clothed them in purple and hung from their neck ornaments of gold.

Alexander announced to the sages that he wanted to go to Africa.—You cannot, for the mountains of darkness will stop you, they responded to him.—That is not enough for me to give up going. Is it about going that I asked your advise? Tell me rather what to do to go there.—Take Libyan donkeys that can travel in the dark, and coils of rope that you will fasten on the side of the route. This will help you on the way back.

He followed their advise and left. He came to a village inhabited only by women. He wanted to engage in combat against them, but they said to him: If you massacre us, people will say that you have massacred women. If it is we who kill you, it will be said that a king has been killed by women. He then said to them: Bring me bread. They brought him a bread of gold on a table of gold.—Do human beings eat bread of gold? he wondered.—If you wanted ordinary bread, does it not exist in your region that you had to come here to seek it? In leaving, he wrote on the gate of the city: I, Alexander of Macedon, I was a fool before having come to this country of women in Africa and having received their advise.

On the way back, he sat next to a spring and ate some bread. He had with him some salted fish. As he rinsed it, it gave off an agreeable smell. It is proof that this spring comes from the Garden of Eden, he said. According to some, he ascended the length of the spring up to the entrance of the Garden of Eden. He arrived and said: Open the gate for me. One answered him: "It is the gate of the Lord, the just shall pass through it" (Psalms 118:20).—I am king, I am an important man! Give me something, said Alexander. One gave to him an eyeball.

He weighed against it all his silver and all his gold, but the entirety did not weigh as much as the eyeball.

—What is happening? Alexander asked the rabbis.

—It is a human being's eye, which is never satisfied.

—How do you know that it is thus?—Cover it with a little dust and it will become light, for it is said: "The day of death and the abyss are insatiable; the eyes of man equally" (Proverbs 27:20).

Rabbi Hayya taught: Whoever studies Torah at night is face to face with the Shekina,[3] for it is said: "I have the Lord constantly before my eyes" (Psalms 16:8), and also: "Arise, cry out at the entry of the night watch . . . in the presence of the Lord" (Lamentations 2:19).

Rabbi Eleazer said in the name of Rabbi Haninah: The disciples of the sages increase peace in the world, thus it is written: "All your children are disciples of the Lord, and great shall be the peace of your children" (Isaiah 54:13).

The meeting between Alexander of Macedon, Alexander the Great, conqueror and master of an empire, in whom political thought must be thought through to the end—or at

---

[3] *Shekina* is the "presence" of God; it is a feminine noun in Hebrew.

least to one of its excesses—, and the "elders of the Negev," as his Jewish interlocutors are called in our text, has seemed to me, in the remarks exchanged such as the doctors of the Talmud understand them or intend them logically, to merit the attention of these final hours of our colloquium.

Of course, the text of the page which has been distributed to you should not be taken for a document attesting to the historical authenticity of the words it relates, nor also for some proof of the real fact of the meeting from which they have been taken. It is the lesson expressed by this venerable fragment—whatever may be the date of its redaction—that is our primary interest today and which we are now going to attempt to approach.

We begin the reading:

Alexander of Macedon posed ten questions to the elders of the Negev [the south].

[1] He asked them if the distance is greater from heaven to earth than from east to west. They answered: From east to west it is greater. You know that when the sun is in the east, everyone to the west can look at it, and when it is in the west, everyone to the east can also look at it. Whereas when the sun is in the middle of the sky, no one can look at it.

The noontime sun at the summit of the heavenly firmament blinds us, for it is too near to our eyes. Even though the light of the sun which rises and sets in the east or west softens and suits the view, traversing distances which would be superior to the heights of the cosmos. The universe is shorter in elevations than in lengths. Are these a childish optics and logic? Does Alexander's question which would like to compare quantitatively the dimensions of the universe testify to no maturity at all? Does it not proceed from some concern of the man of action? Does one not hear in it the preoccupations of the power as also the politics of the man of State, of the conqueror crossing or hollowing out the paths of the universe? Of a politics driven to imperialism, to couriers bearing far away the decisions of the commander in chief and the central administration? But already all the importance of the horizontal in the daily march of human multitudes, toward their place of work. Next to or behind the march of military columns.

Priority of horizontal lines, those of efficiency, and, despite distances and obstacles, the whole marvel of paths, tracks, roads—ways, and hence spirit. The vertical, the elevation to the heavens, only contemplation tends toward this. To know, without movement or grasp. Height, the vertical, is imagination, poetry or dream. Impotent and uncertain movement. There is more meaning, more to do and more to get, more to gain in those horizontal displacements. One succeeds in regulating them by force and by legislation. There would be nothing to get in a contemplative impotence turned toward the heavenly spaces, nothing to learn, except the death of Icarus. The useful height is always very short for man! Hence the first answer to Alexander, which no doubt agreed with the conqueror interrogating the elders of the Negev whom he meets during his very peaceful crossing of the land of Israel. First answer which must flatter the conqueror and the man of State: the horizontal distance decidedly is greater—but also more fruitful—from the Occident to the Orient than that which leads from earth to heaven. First wisdom, wisdom of good sense, wisdom of common sense.

But already a different answer, a repressed answer: that of other sages, sages more sage than the sages, or less sage than the sages, the sages who consult Scripture.

The sages nevertheless think that the two distances are equal, for it is said: "For as the heavens are high above the earth, so His goodness is great for those who fear Him; as distanced as the Orient is from the Occident, so He distances our transgressions from us" (Psalms 103:11).

The verse of the psalm teaches them that the two distances compared are equal to one another. Is not each equivalent to the gap through which God's goodness separates fault from those who fear Him? The sages more sage than the first sages are thus not content with the answer given to Alexander the Great's first question, derived from reasoning about the look which cannot view the noontime sun and which can view it without fear in the evening and morning. The verse of the psalm brings the measures of the world back to another dimension. Pure geometry and pure optics are not sufficient to the veritable evolution of the real and the energies which bear it. Length and height—universe in rectilinear. On the paths of the land, in the streets of the city, dispersed men approach and come toward one another. But already they distance themselves from one another in the clever ruse, in the tormenting hate, in the secret murder of sin. Alienation of human identities, taking distance from themselves in their rupture with others. It is necessary that all this be redressed, redeemed, pardoned, and returned to its just rectitude. Height is necessary for this. The true height is that elevation in the goodness which reestablishes the peace troubled across relations between men. The metaphor of this height has other meanings than that of geometry. It is here that one can think about God. The grace of God is not a scornful glance from high to low, responding to the impotent look of low to high. It is all the strength of a mercifulness that "dis-alienates" consciences distant from themselves. It brings men together. And, in this sense, the measure from earth to heaven must equal that which goes from east to west. Psalm 103:11 affirms this in evoking transgressions. Divine goodness would have all the height necessary for its rays to be able to equalize the expanse of the itineraries of men exposed to sin. Will not Alexander the Great show himself sensitive, at the end of our text, to the perfumes of paradise, he who will have traveled so many forbidden paths?

But only the first version of the answer given by the sages to the first question of Alexander, the one which invokes the argument of the noontime sun inaccessible to sight, is communicated to the Macedonian conqueror.

Meanwhile, from whence comes—following the second version—this blinding brilliance?

Why can no one look at the sun when it is in the middle of the firmament?

Answer:

Because absolutely nothing obstructs the view.

Nothing is interposed between the sun and our eyes. That the sun could not be looked at would not even prove its proximity, but a perfect emptiness, which allows passage to all the rays of solar heat. Height does not have a geometrical grandeur. The astronomical heavens are empty of gods. And our airplanes and rockets will come tomorrow to traverse and conquer it.

Second question:

[2] What has been created first, the heavens or the earth? Answer: the heavens, for it is said: "In the beginning, God created the heavens and the earth" (Genesis 1:1).

Response straightaway referred to a verse of the Bible!

The question of Alexander the Great, disciple of Aristotle, who, beyond the metaphysical alternatives—creation or eternity of the world—, asks about the original meaning of being

as being. Does everything arise from the earth? Does everything descend from heaven? Must one have humility for being
to be, or must one, even before being, have already surpassed
its condition? The answer is straightaway referred to a verse.
The heavens *et cetera.* Without doubt the heavens are mentioned first. And one can recognize in the sages who decide
thus, the School or the House of Shamai, opposed to the School
or the House of Hillel. It is perhaps interesting to recall here
the debate between Hillel and Shamai, which traverses and
"builds" and structures rabbinical thought. Both Schools are
the Word of the living God. Their disagreement would in no
way signify any finitude in revealed wisdom. It signifies the
life of the Torah, what the Talmud calls the war-between-
sages or between "disciples in wisdom." The innumerable
sides of the absolute Truth live in the bosom of rabbinical
debates or disputes, avoiding dogmatism, avoiding heresies.
The House of Hillel, contrary to that of Shamai, teaches us
that the earth was created first. Thus the verse of Genesis
2:4 means: ". . . on the day when God has made earth and
heaven . . .", the earth is named first. The sages of Israel rec-
onciled the two Houses by citing Isaiah 45:12: "And my right
which has stretched out the heaven and my hand which has
founded the earth"—the Creator working with his two hands
has made at the same time heaven and earth. The elders of
the Negev answered, like Shamai, as radical spiritualists.
Think what you want, Alexander the Great said nothing. He
was without doubt a spiritualist!

Third question:

[3] *He asked them: What has been created first, light or
darkness? One answered him: This question has not yet been
decided.*

Light or dark first, a question certainly more radical than
the question relative to heaven and earth. An alternative

deeper than the alternative of spirit or matter. A question which is posed for spiritualism itself. What does one understand after all by spirit? For this, there would have been a refusal to answer! I think that the above refusal does not indicate only the embarrassment which results from a still premature question.

That the creation of light presupposes a previous dark and consequently the birthright of darkness, but that darkness only has meaning in the clarity of spirit, is perhaps the whole problem here, "the question which is not yet decided" of the possibility or the impossibility of the Irrational. Already, to be recognized, it knocks at the gates of Reason, and through this even retracts its unreason, but nevertheless it remains outside knocking.

In our text a less paradoxical and less profound level of this situation is also manifest. The question posed is not resolved, say the elders of the Negev. The wherewithall for the solution is not adequate for discussion in public, nor can there be at all times metaphysics or Kabbalah. The Kabbalah is still not, as in Paris,[4] everybody's affair! Ultimate questions are treated in discreet dialogues and even in the thought of one person alone. Political intelligence, however, perhaps cannot go beyond certain limits. Beyond, it is bad for that intelligence and dangerous for politics.

Our text again remains at this level of prudence when it explains the refusal to answer which the elders of the Negev oppose to the third question of Alexander the Great.

Why did they not answer him that it is the darkness that came first? The elders thought that Alexander was about to

---

[4] Or Hollywood!

*ask them questions about what is below, what is behind and
what is before.*

Does not the Bible indeed tell of the *creation* of light, which
would indicate the anteriority of darkness? But the elders
kept quiet. They knew that they would never finish if they
entered into such questions.

Kabbalistic questions. Infinite questions in these allegedly
ultimate questions. But why were the elders of the Negev
not on their guard earlier?

*But in that case they should not have answered the ques-
tion about the heavens! At the start, they believed that he just
happened upon that question and that he would not pose others of the same type. When he posed the question about light
and dark, they decided to no longer answer, for fear that he
would come to ask them, indeed, what is above and what is
below, what is interior, what is exterior.*

In this interlude there is motivation for the sage's silence,
there is the aristocraticism of true knowledge and of the true
problem despite a concern for universality. There is also
distrust regarding a politics which claims to do philosophy.
Necessity for a secret thought, not to protect itself from ma-
levolence and conspiracies, but due to its subtlety, which renders it fragile and intends it to be discreet. Fear regarding
the non-initiated who interrogates, and of course the reserve
of authentic thought regarding what necessarily remains vul-
gar in journalism. Precaution of authentic thought smitten
with fundamental truths and conscious of the rigors and refined concatenations of their study. Distrust regarding what
menaces this difficult thought in indolent curiosity and in
vulgarization.

Fourth question:

[4] He asked them: What is the definition of the sage? They answered him: The sage is he who foresees what will happen.

The sage, in the lived present, would see what will happen. He reads the *after* by deduction in the *now*, in perception, without giving himself up to the obscure presentiment of an uncontrollable divination. Answer of the elders of the Negev who envisage the entire rationalism of the Occident!

[5] He said to them: Who do you call strong? They said: He who masters his evil inclination.

Evil inclination which would be the passionate deployment of beings in their very individuality, consequently one *against* another—the battle for life! And the human person: he alone who is capable of opposing to his evil inclination, mastering the individual in himself, a force, thus stronger than all forces, a force which defines strength.

That was the fifth question. Here is the sixth:

[6] He said to them: Who do you call rich? They answered: he who is content with the share which is allotted to him.

Admirable stoic principle! Alexander the Great's fourth, fifth and sixth questions—questions attributed to Alexander by the text upon which we are commenting—are literally taken from pages 10a and 10b of the talmudic tractate *Avot* [Fathers]. We know that the recitation of this tractate of six chapters belongs, under the name *Pirke Avot—Wisdom of the Fathers*—to the Shabbat ritual during the weeks which stretch from Passover to the first day of the month of Elul, which in Jewish piety opens the liturgical season of the examination of conscience and of repentance.[5] The answers to

---

[5] The six chapters of "Wisdom of the Fathers," are studied one chapter each Sabbath from after Passover to the start of the month

these three questions are also taken from *Pirke-Avot*, except for the fourth question. The sage is not defined in *Pirke-Avot* as knowing beforehand what will happen. There he is called "he who, in the other—in all men—, finds the opportunity to learn." We will return to this difference. What seems to us important to underline first is the very possibility of hearing from Alexander the Great's mouth questions belonging to the problematic and to the spiritual atmosphere of *Pirke-Avot*, without this prestigious interlocutor having to contest the philosophy of the elders of the Negev on these three essential points, even though in what follows he will show himself closed to certain evidences of those whom he interrogates. Are we thus at a certain stage of Jewish thought—or of Western thought—in which the disciple of Aristotle appears already open to the Torah's voice or spirit, and, at least in the case at hand, in which he would already understand all that the marvel of the human person can illuminate in the unforeseeable tyranny of blind forces, or all that a person's moral will can oppose to irreversible passion, to the unlimited attraction of gold, and to the incessant temptations of good fortune?

Unless this spiritual rapprochment between the world of Alexander and the world of Israel be, despite everything, less advanced than it seemed to us. Alexander did not understand Israel's remark relative to the wisdom which would come to a man from whomever he meets, which would come from

---

of Elul (September/October), the month during which *Rosh Hashanah* (New Year) and *Yom Kippur* (Day of Atonement) take place. This Talmudic tractate is unusual for several reasons: it is made up exclusively of *Mishnah*, without *Gemarah* exposition; it contains no formal *halakic* discussion; and it is made up entirely of ethical teachings.

every man, who already teaches through his being-a-man. Paradoxes, but also the Torah's message, to believe *Pirke-Avot*, forgotten as if by accident in the answer to the fourth question. Wisdom was defined to Alexander only as deductive thought, as science which masters the future. Wisdom— reasonable thought, to be sure, the ideal of the West which does not like the unforeseen, admires strong characters and is capable of despising riches; but which also remains sensitive to the nobility of the conquering sword and will never have peace. It is at the end of the page commented upon that the great Alexander will learn to learn from all men; and even from a whole city of women!

Must we underline the current relevance of this difference between rationality, "reading the future in the present," and the wisdom which still learns from every new human face? In the first, the sage is exposed to ideology, to the abstractions of totalitarianism; it can lead from "scientific socialism" to Stalinism. The sage of the second wisdom is not immobilized in a system, resists cruel abstractions, can be renewed, and is open to each new encounter.

Seventh question:

[7] He asked them: What should one do to live? Kill oneself.—And what should one do to die?—Let live.

Dying proposed as leading to life and living as leading to death, a paradoxical knowledge at first view, and which makes no sense unless living and dying are understood at once literally and figuratively. Living in the alleged plenitude of ventures and joys, living a life said to be intense with appetites and ambitions, battles and rivalry, is to live a dangerous life, a short life—it is to die. Wearing life out, which precipitates death. And death which is not the end of life, but the name given to a whole life of prudence and reserve,

of circumspection—timid life at home, tranquil and medio-
cre life—it is perhaps a long and healthy life. Unless dying
means humbling oneself and hence avoiding jealousies and,
in the shadow, surviving the intrigues of the malicious and a
pitiless mode of life; and living comprises pretensions and
pride and therefore enemies and dangers and death.

But without doubt the remarks exchanged between
Alexander the Great and the elders of the Negev mean to
say more than this. That dying could lead to living, is without doubt to affirm that life, for humans, has meaning only
beyond the egoism of its biological reality, that straightaway
it is life with others, already beyond its perseverance in existing, beyond the "at all costs" of the *conatus essendi*.[6] It is the
affirmation that this human life, its relations with others—
such as they are, with ruptures and resumptions—, is already
love; that love is already self sacrifice going in its essential
intention right up to dying for another. It is this unavowed
intention which animates the kindnesses of human beings
between themselves. So this is the dying that renders living
possible. And this is the dying that requires all the forces of
life to take up this wager of dying.

This humanity of man inseparable from sacrifices, and this
way of committing one's life right up to death in reaching the
human condition, is certainly an ancient idea of the elders of
the Negev and the Community of Israel. "How do we know,"
says a talmudic text (*Berakot* 63b) "that the teachings of the
Torah are only followed by those who are capable of dying for
these teachings, if this is not the text of a verse (Numbers

---

[6] *Conatus essendi*, meaning "perseverance in being," is a term
used by Spinoza to refer to each and every entity's inertial "effort"
to maintain itself as it is, to continue to be, to persist in being.

19:14): 'This is the Torah: the man who dies. . . .'" Defining the Torah—the whole charter of the human—by "a man who dies" is only possible thanks to a midrashic reading of the verse. The inner certainty is here so profound that it is meant and given in the letter of the text, but fortuitously. The plain meaning of the verse in question might as well be saying something else: "This is the Torah (this is the law), the man who dies in a tent and whoever comes into this tent shall be impure with everything the tent contains, etc. . . ." The Midrash permits isolating and reading the first six words[7] by themselves: "This is the Torah, the man who dies."

Eighth question:

[8] He asked them: "What should one do to be popular?"

Answer:

Hate power and authority.

So he retorts:

I have a better answer than yours. One must love power and authority and take advantage of them to do favors for the people.

Question and answer and retort of he who questions the answer he has received. The sole retort in this entire set of questions, which would indicate an acquiescence to the answers given thus far.

The problem of popularity which Alexander introduces by his question testifies that in his eyes political authority implicates a power irreducible to the attractions of the Good in itself, irreducible to an ethical dynamism such as that, for

---

[7] The phrase is made up of six words in the original Hebrew.

example, which fills the values evoked at the start of the dialogue. Alexander would stoutly think that political authority harbors by essence a nucleus of irreducibly arbitrary tyranny, like that denounced by the prophet in Samuel I, 8:11–17.[8] Alexander the Great wonders if this essential royal violence could not nonetheless be made pleasant through some seduction like that which he himself proposes as a "better answer." The answer of the elders of the Negev consists in refusing precisely tyranny, even if pleasant, and in reserving the supreme popularity for the hatred of this irreducible tyranny and the State that appeals to it. This is perhaps the central moment of our entire dialogue.

This negative answer could in no way signify that, for Israel—and for these elders of the Negev—, the State is equivalent to anarchy. It would mean that the acceptable political order can only come to humanity by way of the Torah, its justice, its judges, and its learned teachers. Messianic politics. Yearning—extreme and historical attention as a vigil.

---

[8] Samuel I 8:11–17: "And he said, This will be the custom of the king that shall reign over you: He will take your sons, and appoint them for himself on his chariot, and to be his horsemen; and some shall run before his chariot. And he will appoint for himself captains over thousands, and captains over fifties; and will set them to plough his ground, and to reap his harvest, and to make his instruments of war, and the instruments of his chariots. And he will take your daughters for perfumers, and cooks, and bakers. And he will take your fields, and your vineyards, and your best olive yards, and give them to his servants. And he will take the tenth of your seed, and of your vineyards, and give to his officers, and to his servants. And he will take your menservants, and your maidservants, and your goodliest young men, and your asses, and put them to work. He will take the tenth of your sheep: and you shall be his servants." *From The Jerusalem Bible* (Jerusalem: Koren Publishers, 1992), 333.

Hatred of tyranny, which always "in-nervates" political power. Mistrust and great strictness regarding an order irreducible to the necessities issuing from reason—theoretical or practical—, irreducible to the necessities which are consistent with the freedom of persons, which in the final account are the sources of this freedom. Hatred which the rabbinical commentators (figuring in the margins of the text upon which we are commenting) interpret as nursed against the friends of the men of power, as hatred born against this friendship, which would only be made up of flattery and informing, zone of all corruption. But a hatred that can be understood in a deeper way, as a high degree of criticism and control regarding a political power unjustifiable in itself, but to which a human collectivity, through its very multiplicity—while yearning for better—, is pragmatically obligated. Merciless criticism and control through which this actual political authority, unjustifiable but inevitable, can exercise its actual power. But an always revocable and provisional power, subject to incessant and regular modifications. Is it not thus, in this refusal of the politics of pure tyranny, that the outlines of democracy take form, that is to say, a State open to what is better, always on the alert, always renovating, always in the process of returning to the free persons who delegated to it their freedom subject to reason without losing their freedom? And the excessive word "hatred"—hatred of power and the political authority of constraint—does it not signify the democratic State as being precisely an exception to the tyrannical rule of political power which, according to the elders of the Negev, would merit only hatred? But what a difficult path! What laborious logic!

One quite understands then Alexander the Great's retort. He proposes a "better solution." He maintains a State which rests on an imperative of tyrannical constraint exterior to the attraction of the values on which the elders of the Negev would seem to agree with him. But from this, beyond the resources of political power, he thinks he can obtain the popular favor which is necessary to him through the mediation of philanthropists who "frequent ministers" and whom the elders of the Negev admit detesting. These friends, philanthropists, attentive to popular afflictions, would know how to determine a "politics of social progress." The State capable of beneficent effects would thus struggle on grounds devoid of generosity. But can the great conqueror here lack realism? Perhaps the notion of the Satanic which his interlocutors will evoke in concluding the dialogue attests as much to the philosophy of history as to thought attached to the twists and turns of immediate success.

Ninth question:

[9] Is it better to live on land or on sea?—On land, because all those who risk going to sea only regain their tranquility when they have landed on firm land.

On sea—happy up-rooting of freedom, the spirit awakened by the unknown, by the variation of points of view upon the waves, by the encounter with the other man. Let's not renounce the sea! Then, an alternative: security, quietude of the uncontested truths of the firm ground and risks and perils and marvels of adventure and discovery. Alternative which certainly does not exclude the synthesis of its terms in the destiny of a Europe seeking itself, a universe established between men and nations and heavens and earth. But also a Europe forever anxious without peace, frightened by its dreams and its weapons. The need for firm earth and peace dominates the infinite promises of adventure and historical

movement. Beyond "its creative duration"—how wonder-
ful the tranquil hellenistic conclusion of the "one must stop!"
Reasonable choice which the elders of Israel in the Negev
make.

Tenth question:

*[10] Who among you is wisest?—We are all equal, since we
have all answered your questions as one man.*

Does human intelligence allow itself to be thought as the
excellence of a particular? General reason must start with a
human assembly and must be able to connect with others
and with universality. It participates in the glory of the
genus.[9] Intelligence is by essence teaching and is nourished
by its very communication. Students' questions are indispensable to the teacher's answer. Such at least is the way of
the Torah, always studied in a group, and between men bent
over the text who do not spare themselves objections, refuta-
tions, attacks, defense—"wars of the Torah" in which father
and son mercilessly confront, repulse and collide with one another. Here, contra all dogmatism, are the dialogues, vehe-
ment as they must be, necessary to the spiritual unity of a
dispersed Judaism. The beginning of the verse of Jeremiah
50:36 whose plain sense is translated: "War upon traffickers
in lies, they shall lose their heads," becomes, in the midrashic
translation of the talmudic tractate *Berakhot* 63b—owing to
the ambiguity of the Hebrew word *"badim,"* meaning "traf-
ficker in lies" but also "isolated":[10] "Woe betide those who in

---

[9] Although the French text reads *"génie"* (genius), I believe this
may be a typographical error for *"genre"* (genus).

[10] The three lettered root ("b," "d," "m") of the Hebrew word
"badim," meaning "lies," and the three lettered root ("b," "d," "d") of
the Hebrew word *"bedad,"* meaning "isolated," are both built upon
the same two letter root ("b," Hebrew *"bet"*; and "d," Hebrew *"dalet"*).

Torah study isolate themselves, they shall become stupid."
Eleventh question:

[11] Why do you oppose us?

Why this eleventh question? Would we have badly identified and badly counted the questions announced as ten questions at the start? Unless this question that we find eleventh
derives from the answers given to the first ten questions and
thus serves in some way as the conclusion to the whole dialogue. It might mean: what can the word "opposition" signify
after this conversation which seemed to attest to an agreement on principles between interlocutors, and thus a con-
vergence between the culture of Israel and hellenism? Here
is Israel all ready to enter into the new era called hellenistic
which Alexander the Great's conquests establish. Are we not
intellectually without opposition?

There would be perhaps another way of understanding
this "why do you oppose us?" by recalling the answer of the
elders of the Negev to Alexander the Great's eighth question and the king's retort to that answer. In reacting to the
hatred that they admitted bearing toward authority and political power, he neither contested nor renounced the share
of tyranny that he included in this power. Without doubt, for
him, it indeed innervated power. He had preferred, for "a
better solution," recourse to the mediation of the men who
frequent men invested with power to introduce only thus the
good of the people, in an indirect way, into the exercise of
power. To be sure, he had not scorned this good, and perhaps
he recognized its value in a disinterested and noble way. But
he had not admitted it into the inmost essence of political
authority itself. The opposition between these interlocutors
thus would have retained a rigorously political meaning: "In
the name of what do you oppose the political power which
dominates you?" Why, despite our agreement on all the points

of our dialogue, do you not recognize our victorious march, which—empire that we are—is that of the greatest number? Do you doubt our intention and our political means, which are better than yours, even for assuaging the lot of the unfortunate?

The opposition about which the eleventh question asks can finally mean what Rashi[11] teaches in the commentary adjacent to our text: Why, despite our intellectual agreement, do you close yourself off from our religious beliefs, our polytheistic idolatry which is true for the human majority?

They answered simply: Satan is a conqueror. He is always a conqueror.

Evocation of Satan and his victories in the answer given by the elders of the Negev! Is it not a riposte to the diverse aspects of the question? The intellectual differences which exist between us and others would have become invisible through the ruses of Satan, who is ambiguity itself. It is he who separates thoughts from the cultural context they invoke and from which they come, and mixes ideas. Context which restores the Torah, whose incessant study—vigilance of a thought which seeks the absolute—is the very wakefulness of thought. From here on it is necessary to think of the last lines of our text—we will come back to it—consecrated to the grandeur of the Torah and its study in the general economy of being. Torah which frustrates the diabolical tricks by which the civilizations which rest on truths that rush onward, do not keep their own promises. Or else, in

---

[11] "Rashi" is the acronym of Rabbi Shlomo ben Isaac (1040–1105), foremost Jewish commentator of both Hebrew Bible and Talmud, known for his brevity, clarity and precision. He cultivated vineyards in Troyes, France.

this evocation of Satan, neither his victories nor the political success which he procures, could satisfy wisdom. Success is not proof of ultimate truths!

I can have you executed by a royal decree!—Power is in the hands of the king, but it does not befit a king to lie.

Why this threat which risks brutally putting an end to a conversation conducted thus far in the full freedom of spirit in peace? Would Alexander the Great have found himself the first one attacked in this conversation by the evocation of the Satan to which his victorious power would have been compared or connected? Would he be roused to indignation by the violence of this riposte? Or, short of arguments, would he turn back to the very violence of the tyranny which inner-vates his imperial power? And what is it that then appeases him in the final answer of his interlocutors? Is it the recognition of his power ("power is in the hands of the king")? Or is it the "it does not befit a king to lie," in which the right to violence which was recognized or reproached as his nonethe-less precluded his person from the moral inelegance of lying, as if the verse of Leviticus 19:11[12] proscribing lying could have to do with him despite his barbarity?

Would there not also be—eventuality one evokes with cir-cumspection and under reserve—, in this appeasement, the effect of the hidden virtues of compromise? Recognition ac-corded to the "enlightened tyranny" of a politics consenting to an exchange of remarks and ideas and, in return, the seduction that the ethical order can exert over the pride of power become noble. A discourse is possible with power! Com-promise in the yearning for the absolute order, despite the

---

[12] Leviticus 19:11: "You shall not steal, neither deal falsely, nei-ther lie one to another."

unpleasant likelihood of corruption, totalitarianism, war.

A deep enough appeasement, however, since it becomes the entree of the elders of the Negev to be among the dignitaries of Alexander's empire.

Forthwith he clothed them in purple and hung from their neck ornaments of gold.

But the story or political adventure continues:

Alexander announced to the sages that he wanted to go to Africa.

Already colonial business!

You cannot, for the mountains of darkness will stop you, they responded to him.

The world is not a Euclidean space open to conquest, to the forward movement of a horizontal march. Places inhabited by men concealed under their dissimilarities, whose human look cannot manage to penetrate the night, multiplicity without synthesis, space without transition, without return, exotic worlds requiring, on their paths without destination, the irrational perspicacity of instinct and the guiding threads of the blind.

That is not enough for me to give up going.

This conquering march is probably in the invincible logic of political power, whatever be the limits of that power. Political power wants to expand, it wants to be an empire. Everything that limits it is already against it and provokes it.

Is it about going that I asked your advice? Tell me rather what to do to go there.

Answer:

Take Libyan donkeys that can travel in the dark, and coils of rope that you will fasten on the side of the route. This will help you on the way back.

There would be in this warning of the elders of the Negev the consciousness of a certain gap which divides the world in which the discourse of hellenic-hebraic logic is possible from that of a savage logic toward which one would no longer be guided by light.

He followed their advise and left. He came to a village inhabited only by women.

By women! Humans who would not be men! These are the "natives" of colonial conquests, ever ambiguous faces, under a mask. Human beings who one does not challenge like veritable men. And here among these women—among these humans but not men, among this mass of "natives"—Alexander the Great is taught a lesson. Every man, like a teacher, brings wisdom to a sage, according to *Pirke-Avot*.

He wanted to engage in combat against them, but they said to him: If you massacre us, people will say that you have massacred women. If it is we who kill you, it will be said that a king has been killed by women.

Colonial combat as unworthy of glory! The combat of conquest as unworthy of glory! The imperial passion of the State called to the greatest reservations.

Pacific words of the great conqueror:

He then said to them: Bring me bread. They brought him a bread of gold on a table of gold.

And Alexander:

Do human beings eat bread of gold? he wondered.

They answered:

If you wanted ordinary bread, does it not exist in your region that you had to come here to seek it?

Victorious irony of these women! They know the secret of combats of conquest, as they were able to divine the vigorous dialectic which annuls the glory of these combats. They denounce the politics of a force which is not the mastery of an insatiable desire and of a will to riches which always wants the portion with which the other person makes do.

Remarkable lessons! Lessons well understood by the great Alexander, very brilliant student of Aristotle.

In leaving, he wrote on the gate of the city: I, Alexander of Macedon, I was a fool before having come to this country of women in Africa and having received their advice.

Our text ends. Alexander returns, probably holding onto the rope whose coils he had unwound alongside the paths in going, in order to cross the dimness of his return. He also has bread.

On the way back, he sat next to a spring and ate some bread. He had with him some salted fish.

An amusing picture of Alexander the Great eating salted herring! The same fish he rinsed in the spring water.

As he rinsed it, it gave off an agreeable smell. It is proof that this spring comes from the Garden of Eden, he said.

Alexander of Macedon who dreams of paradise. And of peace. And the first version of our story about Alexander the Great draws to a close with this smell of paradise. There is in this termination of expansion, of Alexander's political violence, a paradisial smell.

But,

[a]ccording to some, he ascended the length of the spring up to the entrance of the Garden of Eden.

The smell is no longer enough for him. He wants paradise itself.

He arrived and said: Open the gate for me. One answered him: "It is the gate of the Lord, the just shall pass through it" *(Psalms 118:20).*

The just, but not the political! Political dignity, the prince's dignity that he has, does not open this gate. He protests in the name of his royal dignity, tyrannical dignity:

—I am king, I am an important man! Give me something, said Alexander. One gave to him an eyeball.

His dignity as a political man, a sovereign, merits a lesson anyway. Would the eyeball that was given to him have a symbolic meaning? He wants to compare, he wants to know what this eyeball is worth. And he weighs it.

He weighed against it all his silver and all his gold, but the entirety did not weigh as much as the eyeball.
—What is happening? Alexander asked the rabbis

who were there. The rabbis, at the gate of paradise, tell him that

—It is a human being's eye, which is never satisfied.

It was necessary to go back again to the eye with which, after all, everything began. Everything began with that look beyond which no one can go, which goes from the Orient to the Occident, with that look which forever sees more of the graspable than the paradisial dreams of those who look toward the height. Here we are back to the first question from among the ten questions posed by Alexander to the elders of the Negev. Alexander asks the rabbis:

*How do you know that it is thus?—Cover it with a little
dust and it will become light, for it is said: "The day of death
and the abyss are insatiable; the eyes of man equally" (Proverbs 27:20).*

Death reduces to its true weight the splendors of the insatiable eye. Must the path from the Occident to the Orient be
more promising than that from earth to heaven? Our text
affirms a radical difference between everything that can have
validity in a reasonable politics, on the one hand, and authentic justice, on the other. That is to say, mercy, charity,
chesid [kindness], which are the fiery furnace of justice, the
Torah which is the source of its flames, and the study by
which this source shoots forth. Justice is opposed to this political desire, born of the insatiable look toward distant horizons, to this infinite taste of politics, this horizontality which
was in question from the start, taken for the essential of existing. Hence we come back to the study of the Torah which
is the principle of peace.

*Rabbi Hayya taught: Whoever studies Torah at night is
face to face with the Shekina, for it is said: "I have the Lord
constantly before my eyes" (Psalms 16:8), and also: "Arise,
cry out at the entry of the night watch . . . in the presence of
the Lord" (Lamentations 2:19). Rabbi Eleazer said in the name
of Rabbi Haninah: The disciples of the sages increase peace
in the world, thus it is written: "All your children are disciples of the Lord, and great shall be the peace of your children" (Isaiah 54:13).*

The verses cited here are very important.[13] It is not only
the intellectual scope of the inquiry to which Scripture gives

---

[13] The words of Rabbi Eleazar, said in behalf of Rabbi Haninah,

rise that they exalt. The study of Scripture is a mode of life which by itself shatters the hard realities of political violence. It brings about the reconciliation of men. Torah—presence of God in the face-to-face, vision of the invisible, peace, thought together.

Synthesis in analyzing. But that is another colloquium.

---

are important enough to be recited every Friday evening as part of the Sabbath liturgy. They derive from an effort to explain the repetition of the Hebrew word for "your children" (*banayok*) in this verse. With different vocalization its letters can be read to mean "your builders" (*bonayek*), indicating that students of the Torah are also builders of peace.

THREE

Who Is One-Self?[1]

TRACTATE CHULLIN 88B–89A[2]

... Raba said: to reward Abraham for having said: "I am ashes and dust" (Genesis 18:27), two commandments were granted to his children: "the ashes of the red heifer" (Numbers 19:2) and the earth of the "spouses suspected of misconduct"[3] (Numbers 5:14). Must one also add the "earth for covering up the blood"?[4] This bears only on a perfecting of the commandment, but to no one's advantage.

Raba also said: To reward the saying of our father Abraham: "from a thread to a sandal strap" (Genesis 14:23), Abraham

---

[1] This lesson was originally given at the thirtieth Colloquium of French-Speaking Jewish Intellectuals, December 11, 1989.

[2] I have consulted *The Hebrew-English Edition of the Babylonia Talmud: Hullin*, trans. Eli Cashdan (London: Soncino Press, 1980), 176–78; and the Brown Judaic Studies translation, *The Talmud of Babylonia: An American Translation, Vol. XXX, B, Tractate Hullin, Chapts. 3–6*, trans. Tzvee Zehavy (Atlanta: Scholars Press, 1993), 277–78.

[3] Though the general and somewhat euphemistic term "misconduct" is used, the rabbis understand that adultery is meant.

[4] *Leviticus 17:13.*

109

gained two commandments: that of the "thread of blue[5] *(of*
tzitzis)"[6] *and that of the "strap of the* tefillin" *(phylacteries).*[7]
For it is said (Deuteronomy 28:10): "And all the peoples will
see that the name of the Lord is associated with you"; apropos
of this there is the teaching: Rabbi Eliezer said: "These are
[the phylacteries][8] *of the head." But what of the "thread of*
blue"? It is taught: Rabbi Meir said: In what does the color
blue differ from all the other colors? Because blue resembles
the sea, and the sea resembles the firmament of the sky, and
the firmament of the sky resembles the sapphire, and the sap-
phire resembles the throne of God; for it is said (Exodus 24:10):
"They beheld the divinity of Israel and under his feet some-
thing similar to the brilliance of sapphire"; and then there is
(Ezekiel 1:26): "It had an appearance of sapphire stone, a
thronelike form. . . ."

Rav Abba said: The theft "consumed" consitutes a difficult
case, for even the perfectly righteous could not restore it. Is it

---

[5] The "thread of blue," part of the *tzitzis* (see note 6 below), is
found in *Numbers 15:37.* The Hebrew for this particular blue is
techeiles. Techeiles is a sky-blue dye made from the secretion of the
amphibian *chilazon* (Hebrew), the precise identity of which is subject to dispute.

[6] *"Tzitzis"* are the ritual "fringes" Jews are commanded, according to *Numbers 15:37–41,* to put on the "corners of their garments."

[7] "Tefillin" are two small black leather boxes containing Scriptural passages (*Exodus* 13:1–10, 11–16, *Deuteronomy* 6:4–9, 11:13–
22), which male Jews traditionally strap onto arm and forehead
during weekday morning services. (It has always seemed to me
amusing but pointless to "clarify" the unfamiliar Hebrew term
tefillin, literally "prayers," with the even less familiar Greek term
phylacteries, literally "watchers" or "guards."

[8] The bracketed insert "[the phylacteries]" here, and the following bracketed inserts in this citation from the Talmud, appear in
Levinas's French original.

not said (Genesis 14:24): "Far be it from me, excepting only what the young men have eaten!"⁹

Rabbi Yohanan said in the name of Rabbi Eliezer ben Simeon: Wherever you hear the remarks of Rabbi Eliezer the son of Jose the Galilean speaking aggadah, lend him an ear open like a funnel. He (Rabbi Eliezer the son of Jose the Galilean) said: It is written (Deuteronomy 7:7): "It was not because you were more numerous than all the peoples that the Lord wanted you." The Holy One blessed be He said to Israel: I wanted you because, even when I granted you greatness, you underestimated yourselves before me. I granted greatness to Abraham and he said: "I am ashes and dust"; to Moses and Aaron and they said: "We are nothing" (Exodus 16:8); to David and he said: "I am a worm and not a man" (Psalms 22:7). The peoples of the world behaved otherwise. I granted greatness to Nimrod and he said (Genesis 11:4): "Let us build a city!"; to pharaoh and he said (Exodus 5:2): "Who is this Lord?"; to Sennacherib and he said (Kings II 18:33): "Which gods of the other nations can he protect . . .?"; to Nebachadnezzar and he said (Isaiah 14:14): "I will ascend to the clouds"; to Hiram, king of Tyre, and he said: "I am a God, I reside in a divine dwelling in the bosom of the seas (Ezekiel 28:2)."

Raba said, and according to others Rabbi Yohanan said: What was expressed by Moses and Aaron is more important than what was expressed by Abraham. For Abraham, the text retains "ashes and dust"; for Moses and Aaron, the text bears:

---

⁹ Genesis 14:23–24: [Abram said:] "I will take nothing from a thread even to a sandal strap, and that I will not take anything that is yours [the king of Sedom], lest you say, I have made Abram rich; far be it from me, excepting only that which the young men have eaten, and the share of the men who went with me. . . ."

"What are we?" And Raba said, and according to others Rabbi Yohanan said: The world subsists only through the merit of Moses and Aaron. From them the value of the words: "We are nothing" [or "What are we?"]. Now, it has been said elsewhere (Job 26:7): "He hangs the earth on nothing." Rabbi Ila'a has said: The world subsists only through the merit of those who when quarrelling are reduced to nothing [bolem: *restrain themselves in the course of a quarrel*]. *For it has been said (Job 26:7): "He hangs the earth over nothingness* (bli-ma).*"*[10] *Rabbi Abbahu has said: The world rests only on he who takes himself for nothing, for it is said (Deuteronomy 33:27): "Underneath [invisible] are the arms of the world."*[11]

To ask ourselves if our life—if the feverish activity which manifests and fills it—still remains the expression of a person, if it responds to the intentions which are authentically ours, in the intersection of multiple causal series, physical, psychic, social, and in the midst of the anonymous forms that convey it, such as heredity, climate, milieu, tradition, media, politics, etc.,—such is without doubt the great question of this colloquium. In human existence, is a person's "as-for-oneself"[12] preserved? Can a person still mean himself and find himself? Does not the very sense of *self* which drives the problem of

---

[10] The text plays between the Hebrew word *bli'ma*, "restraint" (from the three letter root *blm*, "to close up, to restrain") and an interpretation of the same term as if it were made up of the two smaller Hebrew words, *bli*, "without," and *ma*, "anything," i.e., "nothing."

[11] The sense is that those who are underneath, i.e., the humble, are the arms, i.e., the support, of the world.

[12] To call attention to its inner sense, I am translating *"quant-a-*

the "as-for-oneself" require a prior clarification? It is on these points that I am going to interrogate pages 88b and 89a of the talmudic tractate *Chullin*.

> *. . . Raba said: to reward Abraham for having said: "I am ashes and dust" (Genesis 18:27), two commandments were granted to his children: "the ashes of the red heifer" (Numbers 19:2) and the earth of the "wives suspected of misconduct [adultery]" (Numbers 5:14). Must one also add the "earth for covering up the blood"?[13] This bears only on a perfecting of the commandment, but to no one's advantage.*

To understand the notion of the *self* or the *one-self* in order to better distinguish the manner or mode—trace or promise—of the human "as-for-oneself," which risks losing itself under the imbroglio of blind forces, tendencies, and necessities, in which the so-called modern man finds himself or loses himself—that free man or that very busy man—, such will be our effort today. On pages 88b and 89a of the Talmudic tractate *Chullin*, Abraham, "our father,"[14] already since Genesis 17:4 promoted to "father of a multitude of nations," already, therefore, patriarch of the universal humanity, sees *himself* and calls *himself* "dust and ashes" (Genesis 18:17). A notion of a "one-self" which thus would be revealed, if one can say

---

soi" somewhat literally as "as-for-oneself." It could also be translated as "dignity" or "reserve," in the sense that we speak of a person "standing on his or her dignity," with a slight hint of standoffishness.

[13] *Leviticus 17:13.*

[14] In Jewish holy texts and tradition Abraham is known, in Hebrew, as *"Avraham avinu,"* literally "Abraham our father." As the first Jewish patriarch, father of Isaac, grandfather of Jacob, he is literally the father of the Jewish people (and, through Ishmael, the father of the Arab peoples as well).

it, by Abraham's self "introspection" without complacency; the somewhat "adventitious" truth cast by Abraham upon himself in the course of a thought turned toward *the absolutely other other*, preoccupied with the other and proceeding from a care for the other. Prayer of Abraham on behalf of the perverse Sodom threatened with just sanctions by the Lord, prayer by means of a sublime and famous bargaining, lasting ten verses (Genesis 18:23–32), with God himself, a very firm pleading in favor of Sodom before the Creator of the world, disputing about the notion of divine justice. It is precisely here that Abraham declares himself "ashes and dust": "Me, dust and ashes" (verse 27). Complaint in which the destitution of the human creature is admitted in the midst of a dialogue conducted nonetheless at the highest level. Destitution which reveals glory! In self-denying, in his dust and ashes, this thought that stays or already is as-for-oneself, abnegation, there is an elevation of the human creature to another condition, to another level of the human who, authentic under the incessant threat of his mortality, remains someone who thinks of the safekeeping of others. The talmudic doctor Raba, on our page of *Chullin*, tells of the divine reward Abraham won for the words "me, ashes and dust": two comandments. They came to be added to the lot of Sinaic obligations which await Israel. Abraham's descendants are thus gratified through the merit of Abraham their father! But from this perhaps also, in principle, all the descendants of the patriarch, "father of multiple nations," father of the whole of humanity.

Rituals as rewards! One is known as the commandment of the "red heifer" (Numbers 19), the other will be that of the "wives suspected of misconduct," expounded at Numbers 5:19. The Bible describes the ceremonial which is imposed on every husband in Israel who has reasons for suspecting his spouse of infidelity. An odd choice perhaps to include among the 613 possibilites offered by the total number of Torah command-ments,[15] to lay the foundations of a regenerated humanity.

To be sure, one can also be astonished that imperative re-ligious obligations can play the role of rewards. But in the axiology of the Torah, the *mitzvah*, the divine commandment of the Law, does not reduce to an oppressive grip exerted upon the freedom of the faithful. It signifies, even in its con-straining weight, all that the order of the unique God already provides for participation in his reign, for divine proximity and election, and for accession to the rank of the authenti-cally human. As if the "let us make a man" of Genesis 1:26 would have left and still leaves the unfinished. In the appar-ent sub-ordination of obeying God, the freedom of the as-for-me is still to take place.

One can also ask about the intimate relations which, ac-cording to Raba, would exist between the wisdom or the worth of the "me, dust and ashes," on the one hand, and each of the two commandments granted in reward, on the other. Raba remains mute on this point. But the givens of the question and the horizon of spiritualism they prompt seem suggestive to us. The performance of the *mitzvah* of the "red heifer" would hark back to the preparation of the "water of sprinkling"[16]

---

[15] Although there are no doubt more, and rabbinical authorities disagree regarding which they are, the number 613 has tradition-ally been assigned (Makkos 23b) to indicate the number of Torah commandments. These are further broken down into 365 prohibi-tive commandments, corresponding to the number of days in a year, and 248 performative commandments, corresponding (according to tradition) to the number of organs and limbs of the human body.

[16] The "water of sprinkling" (Numbers 19:9, 19:13) is the purify-ing water made from the ritually burnt ashes of the red heifer. It is considered one of the deep "mysteries" of the Torah that this same water which purifies (the one who has come into contact with a corpse) renders its ministering priest impure.

necessary to complete the purification ritual incumbant on those who would have rendered themselves impure by contact with a dead body. The successive points of this preparation are indicated by Numbers 19: finding the animal, a red cow, completely red, undamaged, with no blemish, and which has never borne a yoke, immolation of the animal, its reduction to ashes, mixing the ashes with water. Practical details which without doubt admit of multiple symbolic significations, and which are not explained right away in the eyes of more or less rushed and always insufficiently initiated interpreters. Must one think then of some survival from the magical world? It is indeed not without reason that the commandment of the "red heifer" feeds a tradition of rabbinic humor: the chapter connected with the red cow would belong to the program of Satin. When the devil intends to trouble the faith of Israel, he cites and comments on chapter 19 of Numbers.

Be Satanic eloquence as it may, without doubt it would be more prudent to seek to comprehend the "contact" with a dead body presented as the origin of impurity by starting with a psychology less peculiar, less specialized than magic. Contact with a dead body is always a shock quite sufficient to recall death itself in its negativity without discrimination or exception: the death always already my death. Already to think about death overturns the natural and habitual equilibrium of our values; it troubles the moral order that this equilibrium supports or expresses. The notions of the pure and the impure thrust themselves upon reflection, independent of any superstitious or mystical recollection. Impurity is the name of an always already sordid egoism, which death—my death—awakens like an ultimate wisdom. That the consciousness of being "dust and ashes" does not estrange

Abraham from his disinterestedness, from his care for the other—near or far—, that all the true values remain true for him, despite the death for which everything is the same, this is the purity of the truly human humans of whom Abraham is father. As if henceforth, and by the simple fact of his humanity, the patriarch were the source of a water which purifies, promised, to all his descendants, across the *mitzvah* of the "red heifer," whatever the place, in the recipe of this water, the red heifer deserves. The red heifer remains the symbol of this purification in its rustic traits, perhaps in this way capable of bringing purity or altruism closer to material duties to the neighbor, which are essential to Spirit. A new humanity, a biblical humanism. Without suppressing death, victory won over death! It is Abraham, "dust and ashes," who has won the victory for his children, for Israel, for the "numerous nations," and for all the humanity of humankind.

The second reward that for the benefit of his descendants Abraham merited through his elevation in the humility of the "me, ashes and dust," would have been the commandment of Numbers 5:15 to 5:31 concerning the husband who suspects his spouse of misconduct. The jealous husband, according to this commandment, must take hold of or alarm the sanctuary priest; the suspected spouse is compelled to enter into a ceremony which recalls an ordeal. It takes place within the temple precincts where the wife, to exculpate herself, will say "amen" to the indicting questions, adjurations and threats of the priest, and to a whole series of symbolic gestures in which the Name of the Lord is pronounced. She then consumes the "bitter waters of malediction," a mixture of temple holy water and a handful of earth skimmed from the dust of the sanctuary floor. Guilty, the wife comes to waste away in her body; innocent, she will remain unscathed and promised numerous childbirths. That the familial hearth finds itself destroyed or appeased is of no importance: one must be rid of the ambiguity!

Is there a profound relationship between this style of ordeal and that of the very humble and very high word about dust and cinders wherein Abraham recognized himself and which the law regarding the test of the suspected spouse would reward? The Gemorah affirms it, finding dust and ashes again in the handful of earth cast into the "bitter waters" which the suspected wife drinks. It is a hint that at first sight seems purely accidental and wholely exterior. The Gemorah indeed asks itself if, on this account, even the commandment which orders covering over with earth the spilt blood of a slaughtered animal, evoked at the beginning of our talk, was not also a third reward for Abraham's glorious humility. Gratuitous supposition. But how forget the articulations of the thought which this very hypothesis raises in a subtle talmudic reflection attentive to all that is un-said which resonates in the said! The link between Abraham's thought and the test of the wife suspected of misconduct seems to me profound.

To be sure, "me, dust and ashes," I am capable of caring about the other. My death would not enclose me in myself and kill my loves or my relations to the other. But is love itself really altruist? Is "as-for-me" entirely made of grace? Is it not already concupiscence or within the essential ambiguity of eros? A call to another purity beyond bourgeois prudence?

Is this *as-for-me* entirely made of grace? Is it not already suspect of complacency and, in the essential ambiguity of concupiscence, does it not lack the rigor, elevation and holiness of that which safeguards authentic purity in the controlled and blessed eros of the conjugal union, beyond bourgeois prudential considerations and the customs without principle which tolerate and nourish the amphibology of eros, even, and above all, if they open upon all the splendor of the Western literature of the novel in which love becomes fable and play? The literature of the novel as the perogative of culture, but without doubt at the antipodes from the Torah which is the order of the non-equivocal, where Eros is straightaway recognized in its perturbation and in the depravation of the legal order wherein would arise the very commandment called "the spouse suspected of misconduct," the second reward of Abraham, who was able to say that he is "ashes and dust" without ceasing for all that, in his mortality, to think of the neighbor's salvation.

Raba also said: To reward the saying of our father Abraham: "from a thread to a sandal strap" (Genesis 14:23), Abraham gained two commandments: that of the "thread of blue[17] *(of tzitzis)"*[18] *and that of the "strap of the* tefillin*" (phylacteries).*[19] *For it is said (Deuteronomy 28:10): "And all the peoples will see that the name of the Lord is associated with you"; apropos of this there is the teaching: Rabbi Eliezer said: "These are [the phylacteries] of the head." But what of the "thread of blue"? It is taught: Rabbi Meir said: In what does the color blue differ from all other colors? Because blue resembles the sea, and the sea resembles the firmament of the sky, and the firmament of the sky resembles the sapphire, and the sapphire resembles the throne of God; for it is said (Exodus 24:10): "They beheld the divinity of Israel and under his feet something similar to the brilliance of sapphire"; and then*

---

[17] See note 5 above.
[18] See note 6 above.
[19] See note 7 above.

*there is (Ezekiel 1:26): "It had an appearance of sapphire stone,
a thronelike form. . . ."*

Raba invokes two other remarkable words of Abraham,
pronounced during a war to which the Canaanite kings were
given over (Genesis 14) and in which, accompanied by the
"faithful of his house," Abraham—who was still only *Abram*—
intervened in order to rescue his nephew Lot who had been
captured "with his goods" during an aggression. Abraham
rescues his kin and thus assures victory to the coalition in
which he had fought. But he refuses the plunder offered to
him: "I swear that, from a thread to a sandal strap, I will
take nothing" (Genesis 14:23). Raba tells then of the divine
rewards merited by these noble words. Always commandments and their obligations in the guise of gifts! Instauration of the ritual of the strap: the ritual of the phylacteries,
the role of the *tefillin*, on the one hand, and the ritual of the
thread, the ritual of *tsitsis*, on the other. Rabbi Eliezer the
Great indeed interprets in this sense the verse Deuteronomy
28:10: "All the people of the Earth will see that the Name of
God is associated with yours." This verse obviously would
designate the "*tefillin* of the head" which, attached to the
head of the faithful person, can be seen by everyone around.

That the refusal of plunder becomes the warrior's glory
and is celebrated by a ritual, testifies to a new sense of the
human inaugurated very early in Abraham's life—this is the
escalation of disinterestedness in a conflict, the very idea of
the battle for the Good. What happened to the *tsitsis*? Rabbi
Meir gives a certain orientation to thought: from the blue
colored thread to the celestial height of the divine throne. He
indeed asks how the blue of the *tsitsis* differs from all the
other colors. Going back to the verses of Exodus 24:10 and
Ezekiel 1:26, he glimpses in the blue of the *tsitsis* a gamut of
nuances of this blue reverberating back to the blue of the sea

and, from that, to the blue of the sky and the blue of sapphire stone and, from that, in virtue of the Ezekiel 1:26 verse, right up to the very throne of God.

It is a vision and elevation across the dissimilarities of similarities, a comprehension of spiritual levels across the variations of the sensible. Here meaning is determined as if through the specificity of a blue warm, luminous and of mysterious clarity, different from the forbidden secret of black and from the violent cry of the blazing of red. Blue as blue, essential moment of elevation.

What have we discovered thus far regarding the "as-for-me" of our inquiry? Some allusions which require explicitation, generalization. The Torah is exacting. One must blow on the "ashes" of ideas and images, for the flame tenderly to appear to man. All the same we have gained some traces of a "me" which is affirmed in its devotion to the other and which *is* because it is obligated. Is it without limits?

Rav Abba said: The theft "consumed" consitutes a difficult case, for even the perfectly righteous could not restore it. Is it not said (Genesis 14:24): "Far be it from me, excepting only what the young men have eaten!"[20]

In his renunciation of the plunder, Abraham regrets the impossibility in which he finds himself to restore what the group of the "youths of the house" who accompanied him into battle had used for its upkeep. Consumed pillage. Must one not restore it? Abraham thought that in fact, here, this restitution is impossible and that, consumed, it remains acquired, but that pillage is always to be restored, even if it arose from what constitutes a man's obligation toward his own subsistance as an animal being.

---

[20] See note 9 above.

Abraham's existence, such as Raba understands it, is not pure perseverence in being. With his after-taste of ashes and dust, the consciousness of his mortality, his finitude remains a power, a freedom, a leisure, the dignity of sympathizing and caring for the other man. "As-for-oneself" which recovers mastery and "as-for-the-other." At first glance diminished, but still a force. A force which is no longer physical greatness nor an independent quantity, but which joins in compassion the order of spirit, defines and constitutes it. It is the "as-for-oneself" which discovers itself as "as-for-the-other," presentiment of holiness. This is the marvel proclaimed by the speech or the *aggadah* of Rabbi Eliezer son of Jose the Galilean who is evoked and praised by Rabbi Yohanan in the name of Rabbi Eliezer ben Shimon.

Rabbi Yohanan said in the name of Rabbi Eliezer ben Simeon: Wherever you hear the remarks of Rabbi Eliezer the son of Jose the Galilean speaking aggadah, *lend him an ear open like a funnel.*

What then are these remarks which would be heard without omission?

[Rabbi Eliezer the son of Jose the Galilean] said: It is written (Deuteronomy 7:7): "It was not because you were more numerous than all the peoples that the Lord wanted you." The Holy-One-Blessed-be-He said to Israel: I wanted you because, even when I granted you greatness, you underestimated yourselves before me. I granted greatness to Abraham and he said: "I am ashes and dust."; to Moses and Aaron and they said: "We are nothing" (Exodus 16:8); to David and he said: "I am a worm and not a man" (Psalms 22:7).

Is it a question of humility? Without doubt, and it is already a great virtue, before any analysis. But at the bottom of humility there is the affirmation or discovery of an even higher excellence than that which can be attached to pure complacency in being. There is the glimpse of an excellence of which one feels unworthy and without which the contentment of existing in view of this existing only—the simple "being for being"—would merely be nothingness, as Moses and Aaron designate it at the moment in which the first manna fell from heaven, in the desert, to nourish the people who had left Egypt, famished and already rebellious (Exodus 16:8). Nothingness which in his own way King David knew, feeling under his princely being the crawling subsistance of a worm. It is nevertheless the condition in which pagans delighted without irony, those peoples whose sovereigns are evoked by the speech of Eliezer son of Jose the Galilean, kings who in their own being (where it is only an issue of this very being, as the philosophers say) strive after glory and claim to be divine.

The peoples of the world behaved otherwise. I granted greatness to Nimrod and he said (Genesis 11:4): "Let us build a city!"; to pharaoh and he said (Exodus 5:2): "Who is this Lord?"; to Sennacherib and he said (Kings II 18:33): "Which gods of the other nations can he protect . . .?"; to Nebachadnezzar and he said (Isaiah 14:14): "I will ascend to the clouds"; to Hiram king of Tyre, and he said: "I am a God, I reside in a divine dwelling in the bosom of the seas (Ezekiel 28:2)."

According to another tradition which one attributes to Raba—but also, according to others, to Rabbi Yohanan—however this time without referring to Rabbi Eliezer son of Rabbi Jose the Galilean—, Abraham's formula, "I am ashes and dust," would not merely express the same humility as the formula of Moses and Aaron, "What are we?" There would have been more in the latter than in the former. The total negation would be more radical than that which "ashes and dust" limits. But the disproportion is not merely formal: an entirely new way of transcending or enlarging the "as-for-oneself" of existing appears. To be sure, without ever striving for the greatness of Nebachadnezzar and without envying Hiram, king of Tyre, his divinity—who, both of them, know nothing which would go beyond being—, but also without allowing one to forget the universality of the boundless creature,[21] whether in the eyes of the other man, be it the neighbor. The "What are we?" of Moses and Aaron is a new modulation of the "as-for-oneself": retaining its fire but quitting a quarrel—this is the primordially human! It makes the universe possible, the wholeness of the world. To say this in the language of piety: through the merit of he who restrains himself in a quarrel, the wholeness of being subsists. This is the new signification of the "What are we?" of Moses and Aaron, and the new and fullest meaning of the "as-for-oneself." Peace as the foundation of being. Peace as the meaning of all ontology: the human as the consistancy of the Whole. Perhaps the chaos from whence being has issued, thought of as a primordial quarrel.

Raba said, and according to others Rabbi Yohanan said: What was expressed by Moses and Aaron is more important than what was expressed by Abraham. For Abraham, the text retains "ashes and dust"; for Moses and Aaron, the text bears:

---

[21] *"la creature immense"*—perhaps a reference to the *"Adam Harichon,"* whose measure was huge, from earth to heaven, and from one end of the earth to the other, of the talmudic tractate *Chagigah*? Or to the no less immense *"Adam Kadman"* of the *Shi'ur Qomah*?

"What are we?" And Raba said, and according to others Rabbi Yohanan said: The world subsists only through the merit of Moses and Aaron. From them the value of the words: "We are nothing" [or "What are we?"]. Now, it has been said elsewhere (Job 26:7): "He hangs the earth on nothing." Rabbi Ila'a has said: The world subsists only through the merit of those who when quarrelling are reduced to nothing [bolem: restrain themselves in the course of a quarrel]. For it has been said (Job 26:7): "He hangs the earth over nothingness (bli-ma)."[22] *Rabbi Abbahu has said: The world rests only on he who takes himself for nothing, for it is said (Deuteronomy 33:27): "Underneath [invisible] are the arms of the world."*[23]

A text barely comprehensible in translation, founded in part on verbal similarities which are only visible in the Hebrew text. The "What are we?"—*venachnu ma*—literally signifies: "And us, what are we?" It is related to the *blima*, "without whatever it is," of Job 26:7. And Rabbi Ila'a, in order to to say "he who restrains himself," employs the verb *balom*, "be restrained in a quarrel," which includes the three consonants *b, l, m*, which occur in the term *blima* of Job 26:7. Midrashic steps and liberties whose freedom, intentions, principles and sublime art, it is not the place here to interpret. Freedom which also belongs to the final contribution of Rabbi Abahu, who seems to borrow the last three words of verse 27 of chapter 33 of Deuteronomy in translating one phrase after the other, to obtain "underneath world arms," and to read it as what is underneath (the hidden, the obscure) are the arms of the world (bears the world).

---

[22] See note 10 above.
[23] See note 11 above.

It is a magnificent conclusion to this entire fragment, in which we have looked for some illumination regarding the "as-for-oneself," regarding what is presupposed and implied by the personal act, which comes down to an extreme importance attached by rabbinic thought to the attention one person bears upon another. It is the initiative of a conceding which, in the clash of blind forces, in the quarrel which is perhaps the sense—or the non-sense—of chaos, itself preceding being, already makes the world possible. Being as peace and as founded on the apparently negative movement of restraint. Ontology open to the responsibility for the other.

INDEX

Aaron (brother of Moses), 11, 67,
 111–12, 122–23
Abaye, Rabbi, 68, 70
Abba, Rabbi, 110, 111, 112
Abbahu, Rabbi, 112, 125
Abraham, 4, 9, 46, 110, 114–15,
 117–19, 120
Adam, 4, 10, 37, 38
Adultery, 114–15, 117, 118–19
Aggadah, 14, 40, 111
Akiva, Rabbi, 61, 61n
Alexander of Macedon. *See*
 Alexander the Great
Alexander the Great, 7–8, 79–106
America, 3, 5
Anti-Semitism, 58n14
Aquinas, Thomas, 6
Aristotle, 86, 91, 104
Ark of the Covenant, 8
"Ashes and Dust," man as, 122–25
Athens, 15, 17
Auschwitz, 16

bar Ahbah, Rabbi Ada, 52, 63
bar Issac, Rabbi Nahman, 52, 63, 64
bar Raba, Rabbi, 54, 121, 122, 123
ben Gamaliel, Rabbi Hananiah, 51–
 52, 55, 57, 58–59, 61n, 63, 66
ben Isaac, Rabbi Shlomo, 100, 100n
ben Levi, Rabbi Joshua, 53, 61, 67–
 68, 70
ben Shimon, Rabbi Eliezer, 51, 52,
 52n, 59, 60, 61, 122
Bergson, Henri, 29
Bible (Torah). *See also* specific books
of, such as Genesis.
 analysis of, 26–27, 29, 68, 69–70,
  75–75, 106–07

commandments in, 114–15
and commitment, 93–94
and exegesis, 24, 25, 76
fundamentalist interpretation of,
 25
and humanity, 4
and image of God, 46
Jewish interpretation of, 25, 39,
 68, 69
and Moses, 7
as myth, 14
and oral tradition, 35
Protestant interpretation of, 29–30
secularization of, 63
Spinoza on, 19, 25
study of, 76, 82, 87, 98–99, 100, 107
symbolism in, 10, 30
Talmud on, 25, 34
and Ten Commandments, 7
Biblical humanism, 1, 2–12, 25
Boaz, 54, 68
Buber, Martin, 5, 22, 27n, 44n53
Bultmann, Rudolf Karl, 5

Cainian vision of world, 57
Canaanite kings, 120
Chalier, Catherine, ed.
 L'Herne: Emanual Levinas, viii
Chaos, 125, 126
Civilization, 61–62
Colloquium of French-Speaking
 Jewish Intellectuals, vii, viii,
 69n, 79n1, 109n1,
Colossians, Book of, 6
Conatus essendi (perseverance in
 being), 93, 93n
Concluding Unscientific Postscript
 (Kierkegaard), 17n11